REVISED AND UPDATED THIRD EDITION

FANTASTIC MARKETING 3.0

The Ultimate Playbook
for AI-Powered
Fan Engagement

MEREDITH OLIVER, MIRM, CSP

For information or bulk orders, contact:
meredith@creatingwow.com or call 321-230-1287

www.MeredithCommunications.com

Cover Design, Creative Direction, Meredith Oliver

Cover, Graphic Designer, a Very Talented Designer in Ukraine
Who Prefers to Remain Anonymous

Interior Design by Adina Cucicov

ISBN 978-0-9978260-8-1

AI Disclaimer

Portions of this book were researched and edited with the assistance of artificial intelligence. All concepts, frameworks, examples, strategies, and final decisions reflect the author's original thinking, experience, and expertise. AI was used as an editorial partner, never as a substitute for human judgment, professional insight, or the author's voice.

Also by Meredith Oliver

FANtastic Selling 3.0: The 10 Undeniable Traits of Rock Star AI-Powered New Home Sales Leaders

For Brady.
You are the most FANtastic gift
I've ever received. I am unabashedly your
SUPERFAN, forever and always.

TABLE OF CONTENTS

ABOUT THE AUTHOR

MEREDITH OLIVER IS the founder and chief marketing strategist of Meredith Communications, a digital marketing agency in Raleigh, NC. For over 20 years, Meredith Communications has provided innovative and effective digital marketing solutions for home builders and related companies, including website design, search engine optimization, content marketing, and social media marketing.

Meredith holds a Master's Degree in Corporate Communication and Technology from Rollins College®, a Bachelor's Degree in Psychology from the University of Central Florida®, and the prestigious designation of Certified Speaking Professional®, the highest designation conferred by the National Speakers Association.

Meredith has authored eight books, including the out-of-print titles *Click Power* (1st, 2nd, and 3rd editions), *The Fan Factor*, and *FANtastic Marketing* (1st and 2nd editions).

Currently available in print and eBook on Amazon® are *FANtastic Marketing 3.0: The Ultimate Playbook for AI-Powered Fan Engagement* (3rd edition) and *FANtastic Selling 3.0: The 10 Undeniable Traits of Rock Star AI-Powered New Home Sales Leaders* (2nd edition).

Meredith has been a featured speaker at pivotal industry events, including the International Builders Show (IBS – 24 appearances), The Super Sales Rally (8 appearances), MozCon, the Volkswagen National After-Sales Conference, the Kentucky Society of Human Resources (SHRM), and the Annual Conference and Expo of the National Automobile Dealers Association (NADA – 2 appearances).

She is a member of the National Association of Home Builders (NAHB), the North Carolina Home Builders Association (NCHBA), the Raleigh-Wake County Home Builders Association (HBA), and the Home Builders Association of Durham, Chatham, and Orange Counties (HBADOC).

Her leadership roles have included serving as President of the Carolinas Chapter of the National Speakers Association (NSA), Chair of the NAHB Institute of Residential Marketing (IRM), Chair of both the Communications Committee and the Education Committee of the NAHB Professional Women in Building Council (NAHB PWB), and as a Trustee on the NAHB National Sales and Marketing Council (NAHB NSMC) Board of Governors.

Meredith's dedication and contributions to the home building industry have earned her numerous accolades, including the 2020 Associate Member of the Year from the NC HBA, the 2017 MIRM of the Year from NAHB, the 2016 National Member of the Year from the NAHB PWB, the 2015 Bill Molster Award for Outstanding Service and Lifetime Achievement from the NAHB NSMC, and the 2013 Chapter Member of the Year from the Carolinas Chapter of the NSA.

After enduring intermittent headaches for years, she was diagnosed in the fall of 2020 with a rare, incurable chronic illness known as Intracranial Hypertension (IH). Her number one symptom is a daily intractable headache that rates between 7-9 out of 10 on the pain scale. The daily headache persists to this day, 24/7/365. Despite this challenging condition, Meredith remains deeply committed to her family, her clients at Meredith Communications, and her contributions to the homebuilding industry. She continues to seek treatment and raise awareness about IH, hoping that one day, the daily headache—and the many other persistent symptoms accompanying chronic pain—will subside.

Meredith lives in Raleigh, NC, with her husband, son, and mini-Australian Labradoodle. She is a Florida Gator football fan, an avid reader of spicy fantasy fiction, and a shoe fanatic who loves to geek out over technology and digital marketing almost as much as she likes to shop.

AUTHOR'S ACKNOWLEDGEMENTS

MY EARLIEST MEMORIES involve playing in the basement of our home in Louisville, KY, while my dad operated a printing press, tirelessly cranking out copies of his latest book. He allowed me to doodle on the boxes of books while I pretended to be his "*Secentenary*" (that's how a three-year-old says Secretary), fully immersed in a world of creativity and purpose.

As I grew older, I continued to spend time in his office at the church where he served as pastor, learning how to run the copy machine, create transparencies, and type the weekly newsletter. As a teenager, I taught adult Sunday school classes, laying the foundation for my eventual path as an author and public speaker. **I am profoundly grateful to my parents for fostering an environment where dreams were encouraged and aspirations supported.**

In addition to my parents, **I feel incredibly blessed to have a wonderful brother, Parker Miller**. Both he and his wife, Wade, are exceptional attorneys, but their professional success isn't what I appreciate most. My brother has always encouraged and supported my dreams. I financed a significant portion of graduate school with the winnings from competing in local and state Miss

America Scholarship Pageants®. I remember one Sunday morning after another heartbreaking pageant loss (I placed 1st Runner Up 14 times in a row before winning my first local title, Miss Sanford). My brother listened to my frustration and helped me work through it. He later wrote me a letter titled "The Real Jewels in My Crown," describing my positive attributes as jewels in the crown of life. It was an incredible piece of creative writing that I cherish. In my last year of competition, I placed in the Top Ten in the Miss Florida Pageant®, winning the Talent and Community Service Awards. I wish my parents and brother could have joined me on stage for those awards—we earned them together.

Equally instrumental in my journey has been my husband, Allen Oliver—the CEO and CFO of the Meredith Fan Club. When I called you from IBS and said I wanted to quit my six-figure work-from-home job to start a digital marketing agency for home builders, you didn't choke, blink, or laugh. Instead, you said, "Let's go!" Years later, when I told you I was pregnant with our son and had a fully booked speaking calendar requiring weekly travel, you responded with unwavering enthusiasm: "Let's go!" And most recently, when I revealed that I had been diagnosed with an incurable chronic illness that would be costly to manage and demand so much more from you, you still said, "Let's go!" **Your steadfast belief in me, boundless patience, and unfailing support have never wavered.** I will never stop being grateful to you for the life we've built together.

One of the most significant rewards of a two-decade career is the transformation of **trusted colleagues into cherished, lifelong friends. Kerry, John, Angela, and Melinda** (from her perch in heaven where she is undoubtedly making everyone laugh), your mentorship, unwavering support, and unconditional love mean more to me than words can express. I am forever thankful for our bond.

I also owe so much to the incredible team at Meredith Communications. Over the years, we've weathered the highs and lows of the ever-changing market, surviving challenges like the downturn and crash of the homebuilding industry. You are the reason I remain passionate about digital marketing. **I am privileged to lead a team of such dedicated, talented individuals who pour their hearts into ensuring our clients' success.** To Allen, Chris, Megan, Emmy, Vanessa, John, Jim, Cynthia, and Alison—thank you for your exceptional work, loyalty, and commitment to excellence. Meredith Communications is nothing without you!

PREFACE

I WAS EAGER to set the world on fire when I graduated from the University of Central Florida with a B.A. in Psychology in the late 1990s. Reality hit hard when I realized that a bachelor's degree in psychology wasn't the ticket to the lucrative, fulfilling career I had imagined; instead, an advanced degree was necessary. At that time, I wasn't mentally or financially prepared to start a graduate program, and I found myself working for UnitedHealthcare®, launching the Orlando division. My role as a Provider Relations Representative involved recruiting physicians to join the provider network. Let me tell you: selling HMOs to doctors felt like ramming your head into a brick wall every single day.

The sales pitch was challenging due to the minimal upside for the physician. I couldn't assure the physicians that insurance claims would be paid on time (or at all, for that matter). I couldn't promise that standard fees would be honored. I couldn't guarantee a smooth experience with the HMO because the paperwork was often complicated and repetitive. What could I promise? Numerous frustrated patients who needed immediate care. It was a tough sale; however, after five grueling years, it shaped me into the persistent, tough, and resilient salesperson I am today.

I needed a new career direction and was unsure where to focus. My dad clipped a newspaper ad for a brand-new Master's Degree program. Encouraged by him, I took a leap of faith and enrolled in one of the first Master's programs in the US for Corporate Communications and Technology. He told me, "I think the Internet is going to be a thing." Well, lesson learned—you should always listen to your dad! Sure enough, the Internet became a big deal. Over the past 20+ years, Meredith Communications has helped businesses deploy digital marketing to grow their brands, connect with customers, and achieve remarkable success.

On the first day of graduate school, each student received a Compaq laptop computer that weighed roughly fifteen pounds. Maybe I'm exaggerating, but the Compaq was heavy and symbolic of the challenge ahead. We were told to open the "My Documents" folder to get the notes for class that day. Right away, I thought, *the WHAT folder? Where is that? How does this thing work?* You see, my college years were pre-internet (you know, before the earth cooled and the ice melted). At work, we used mainframe terminals, not personal computers. The upshot was that I knew nothing about laptops, file management systems, Microsoft Office®, or the like. At that moment, it hit me that I had just enrolled in a $40,000+ Master's Degree program in Communication Technology, yet I couldn't operate a basic laptop. Oh my.

I went home that evening inconsolable. I told my husband I was dropping out and begging for the tuition back. Ever the calm one, my husband wrote on a sticky note *C = Hard Drive, A = Floppy Disk* and stuck it to the monitor. He told me the next time an instructor directed me to go to My Documents, I should look for the C.

I sat there staring at that sticky note for several hours, knowing I had a big decision to make. The bottom line is that the laptop stood between me and a future that did not involve selling HMOs to doctors. With the grim specter of selling HMOs to motivate me, I decided to press forward and stay in the class. I tell you this next part *not to impress you but to impress upon you* what is possible when we refuse to quit. Two years later, I graduated with a 4.0 and was voted by my peers and professors as one of two (we tied) Most Outstanding Graduate Students in my class.

Because of my transformational journey, I can ask you: What obstacle stands in the way of your future success? You are in the right place if it's related to sales, marketing, or technology. I can help you because I've been there. **My mission is to help others get unstuck, embrace change, and build the career and lifestyle they most desire.**

As I reflect on my career, I realize I've had a front-row seat to the three most significant and life-changing revolutions at the intersection of **technology, communication, and information**:

1. **The Internet**—Transformed how we access information and introduced the globalization of selling and marketing goods and services.

2. **Social Media**—Democratized communication and redefined how we build connections and communities.

3. **Artificial Intelligence**—I believe it is as transformative as the invention of the Internet itself.

AI represents a monumental leap forward in technology, marketing, communications, and customer engagement. It offers unprecedented opportunities to personalize experiences, automate processes, and unleash creativity at scale. This third edition of FANtastic Marketing focuses on the power of AI and how it can be integrated into marketing strategies to drive unprecedented results.

Thank you for joining me on this journey. Let's dive into AI-powered FANtastic Marketing and make your business unforgettable.

INTRODUCTION

WELCOME TO THE THIRD edition of FANtastic Marketing! In a world where technology and consumer expectations evolve at lightning speed, staying relevant as a marketer or business owner has never been more challenging or exciting. This book is your playbook for navigating those challenges, leveraging cutting-edge tools, and creating a marketing strategy that stands out and builds enduring connections with your fans.

Over the years, I've had the privilege of helping countless businesses, from startups to industry leaders, transform their marketing efforts. I've seen the immense power of engaging prospective customers deeper, building loyalty, and turning them into SuperFans before they buy. But the marketing landscape is shifting again, and this edition embraces the newest game-changer in that evolution: **artificial intelligence (AI).**

The core principles of this book remain unchanged—it is about *creating fans **BEFORE** they buy with a FANtastic Marketing experience (MX).* From creating a wow-worthy website to building a dynamic digital footprint, from harnessing the power of social media to unleashing word-of-mouth magic through online reviews, these timeless strategies form the backbone of any winning marketing plan. However, this edition goes further by **integrating the transformative power of AI** into each of these tactics.

WHY AI MATTERS

I completely understand and relate to feeling very skeptical about AI and wanting to hunker down in a bunker where your identity, loved ones, and content are safe from predators. If you feel or think that way, I get it.

If you believe AI cannot be integrated into your job, you may be correct... but perhaps you're not. Please keep reading. Certainly, there are industries like legal, banking, and healthcare, where we still have much to learn about AI and privacy. This book is designed for sales and marketing leaders primarily working in companies with a Business-to-Consumer model.

In Secret #1, we will explore the importance of curiosity and lifelong learning. Accurately assessing AI (or any emerging technology) requires curiosity. And you can't make a proper assessment without being thoroughly informed. Ignore the late-night comedians' jokes about AI and the quick memes you've encountered on social media. AI may not be what you believe it to be. In this book, you will uncover what you have yet to understand about AI, enabling you to determine how or whether to incorporate it into your daily life. These pages offer a fair and balanced analysis of AI, acknowledging both the possibilities and the pitfalls.

AI isn't just the latest buzzword—it's a revolution. Just as the Internet redefined how we access information and Social Media redefined how we communicate, **AI is changing how we engage, personalize, and create**. Imagine understanding your fans better than ever, automating routine tasks, and generating marketing content that speaks directly to the heart of your audience. That's the promise of AI, and I'm here to show you how to use it effectively.

But this book isn't just about technology. It's about people—your fans. Even as tools evolve, the core principle of **FANtastic Marketing** remains the same: *put your fans first*. Great marketing isn't about flashy gimmicks or slick campaigns; it's about understanding what your customers need and creating an MX before they buy that makes them feel heard, valued, and connected.

WHAT TO EXPECT

This book is divided into five parts, each designed to guide you through creating a marketing strategy that works:

1. **The Pre-Season**—Lay the groundwork with a deep dive into what makes your fans tick and how to build a culture of superfandom.

2. **The Players**—Learn who your fans are, what they need, and how to reach them with messaging that resonates.

3. **Play Ball!**—Explore the ten marketing secrets that will help you step up to the plate, keep your eyes on the ball, and move the goalposts to achieve marketing success.

4. **Charge the Back Nine**—Optimize and measure your efforts with strategies for analytics, conversions, and connecting the dots between online and offline experiences.

5. **Home Field Advantage**—Wrap it all up with tools, summaries, and resources to help you sustain your success.

Throughout the book, you will encounter real-world examples, case studies, practical exercises, tech tool mentions, and insights from my experiences working with home builders across the US. Most examples focus on Business-to-Consumer business models, with a few highlighting Business-to-Business business models. I don't include many eCommerce examples, as that is a separate digital marketing discipline.

LET'S GET STARTED

Marketing today is both an art and a science, requiring creativity, empathy, and the ability to adapt to ever-changing tools and trends. This book equips you with all three. Whether you're a seasoned marketer or just starting, **FANtastic Marketing** will show you how to cut through the noise, earn the loyalty of your fans, and drive measurable results.

The future of marketing is here, and it's more FANtastic than ever. Let's dive in!

Part I

THE PRE-SEASON

"All men are created equal.
Some work harder in the pre-season."

Emmitt Smith, NFL All-Time Leading Rusher,
Three-Time Super Bowl Champion
(And the best running back in Florida Gator history. Go Gators!)

THE FLO EFFECT

I BEAR A STRIKING, uncanny resemblance to Flo the Progressive Girl. With the right hair and makeup, it's almost impossible to tell the difference between me and the much loved, immediately recognizable Flo. I admit the resemblance isn't something I love. In fact, it's quite *awful* for strangers to remark that you are the perfect doppelganger for an over-the-top, larger-than-life, comedic television spokesperson.

All kidding aside, like her or not, Flo, the beloved spokesperson of Progressive® Insurance, has been a household name since her debut in 2008. Portrayed by actress Stephanie Courtney, Flo is an iconic figure in the marketing world. She blends humor, relatability, and a touch of eccentricity to humanize an otherwise dry industry. Hundreds of commercials and years later, Flo remains as relevant as ever, consistently helping Progressive stay at the forefront of the property and casualty insurance market.

What makes the Flo commercials so effective? We love Flo. We can relate to Flo. Given the chance, you probably would have a beer with Flo. Her character puts a friendly face on a not-so-sexy product.

The Flo Effect is more than the character's friendly and relatable communication style. Yes, we like Flo with her perky quips, bouffant hair, and megawatt smile, but we like her because *we perceive she likes us*. Flo is a **superfan** of the Progressive customers in the commercials. She gets what we, the insured, want from our insurance company, and the message in the commercials proves that she *gets* us. We want fair and fast claim service, and Flo understands and validates that concern. We want competitive pricing, and with one swoosh of her price checker gun, Flo demonstrates that Progressive hears that concern and has a solution. Finally, Flo knows we want to bundle and save if we are loyal enough to have multiple lines of insurance with one company.

The Flo marketing campaign demonstrates what I call *The Power of We*.

The character creates a relationship, a WE, in the viewer's mind and instantly transforms the marketing from talking *to* the target audience to talking *with* the target audience. WE feel like Progressive gets what we want from insurance. WE want to know more. WE refer our friends. WE pay attention the next time a Flo commercial comes on or see a digital ad for Progressive. And most importantly, WE buy into the idea that Progressive cares about our needs and has the right solutions to meet those needs. And when WE buy-in, we buy and buy.

But how has Flo's influence evolved in a world where **artificial intelligence (AI)** is reshaping marketing strategies? Progressive hasn't just rested on Flo's charm—they've *supercharged her persona* *by incorporating AI into their marketing efforts.* For example, in 2017, Progressive introduced an AI-powered chatbot featuring Flo's personality to interact with customers on platforms like Facebook® and Messenger. The Flo Chatbot enables users to initiate auto insurance quotes and inquire about insurance-related topics via Facebook Messenger. This innovation positioned Progressive as the first top 10 US insurer to offer such a service on Messenger.[1] In 2020, Progressive enhanced the chatbot by incorporating Flo's voice, creating a more personalized and engaging customer experience. This advancement was achieved through a collaboration with Microsoft, utilizing Azure AI capabilities.[2] **The chatbot doesn't just answer questions; it delivers Flo's trademark wit and reassuring tone, offering a seamless extension of the *Power of We* that makes Flo so effective.**

Imagine the possibilities: a chatbot with Flo's persona can engage with customers 24/7, providing instant, personalized responses that make each customer feel understood and valued. **This isn't just customer service; it's fan-centric marketing at its best.** Progressive uses AI to turn a one-dimensional character into an interactive experience, bringing customers closer to the brand than ever before.

In addition to leveraging AI for engagement, Progressive has integrated machine learning into its broader marketing strategy. By analyzing customer data and behavior, the company tailors its marketing campaigns to individual preferences, ensuring every ad, email, or interaction feels personal. This is a prime example of how AI doesn't replace the human element of marketing but enhances it—just like Flo's friendly demeanor, but now powered by cutting-edge technology.

What can we learn from Progressive's approach? Marketing success isn't just about creating a memorable character—it's about **evolving that character to meet the expectations of a digitally savvy audience**. With AI, Progressive has ensured that Flo remains more than a spokesperson; she's a *fan-centric marketing experience* that keeps customers returning for more.

Are you a superfan of your fans? No matter how much your customers occasionally irritate and frustrate you, do you still love them? If not, it's time to trade your jersey for a job with customers you love and respect.

If you answered yes, do your fans know that? Are your fans aware of how much you respect, care for, and understand their wants and needs? Marketing and sales messages are the primary ways to convey your superfandom; this book will teach you how. Sales and referrals will grow once you learn to communicate this message clearly, concisely, and persuasively. The reward is a multiplier effect; eventually, *your fans will start selling and marketing for you.*

Make no mistake: This is a marketing book, not a customer experience (CX) book. While marketing and customer experience are nearly impossible to separate in today's customer journey, as they are two sides of the same coin, for our purposes in the book, we will focus on *creating fans BEFORE the sale with a FANtastic Marketing Experience (MX).*

Classic customer experience books like *Raving Fans* emphasize delighting and exceeding customer expectations AFTER the sale. I wish to expand this definition because *today's digitally savvy, mobile, and social media-connected customers want to know if you align with their desires and needs BEFORE they buy.* After the sale, it's too late! If your marketing and sales messages don't convince me that you *get* me, I will tune you out and eliminate you from consideration long before I add your product to my Amazon shopping cart, fill out a lead form, or have an in-person sales meeting.

Of course, it's not enough to create a WE throughout the MX only to let them down once they become customers.

Your CX must live up to the promise of your MX.

You'll be cast aside, overlooked, and canceled on social media if it doesn't. Negative reviews will surge, and customer acquisition and retention rates will ultimately decline. We are highly sensitive to fraudulent claims and hollow pitches, crying for attention and failing to deliver. If you believe you can't truly provide the superfan experience, go back to the CX basics until you do.

First, let's examine how Stitch Fix® transformed how we shop for clothes.

STITCH FIX AND THE POWER OF WE

SEVERAL YEARS AGO, I became a SuperFan of Stitch Fix, a subscription-box shopping service that revolutionized how men and women shop for clothes, shoes, and accessories. At that time, subscription boxes became popular as the preferred way to shop for everything from pet supplies to beauty products to craft beer. Among these, Stitch Fix emerged as a standout success story—no wonder why.

"As of the fiscal year ending August 3, 2024, Stitch Fix reported annual revenue of **$1.34 BILLION** and market capitalization at approximately $564.17 million, with an enterprise value of about $434.70 million."[3] Even today, Stitch Fix continues to revolutionize how we shop, blending cutting-edge technology with an intimate understanding of its customers' needs.

Founded in 2011 by Harvard Business School graduate Katrina Lake, Stitch Fix quickly gained fame for combining human stylists with data science. Fast forward to 2024, Stitch Fix launched StyleFile, an

AI-driven tool that enhances the accuracy of its recommendations by creating comprehensive customer profiles, setting a standard for the fan-centric marketing approach this book advocates. This innovation aims to deepen the Power of We, ensuring every interaction feels personal and relevant. For instance, if you rate a floral dress highly in one Fix, you may receive complimentary pieces like a denim jacket or wedge sandals in your next shipment—this exemplifies AI at its finest, paired with the human touch of a stylist's thoughtful note.

Stitch Fix's secret to success isn't its use of artificial intelligence (AI), it's the seamless integration of AI with Human Intelligence (HI).

This powerful partnership ensures every customer interaction feels personal, thoughtful, and highly customized. It's essential to recognize that each interaction isn't just about delivering exceptional service—it's also an MX opportunity to sell more clothing, shoes, and accessories. While this discussion highlights Stitch Fix's customer experience, it also underscores a critical aspect of its marketing strategy: *turning personalized CX into powerful MX moments for future engagement and sales.*

Here's how Stitch Fix works: customers complete a detailed online profile, sharing their size and style preferences, such as what colors to avoid or fabrics they dislike. This profile doesn't just sit on a server—it powers a sophisticated AI engine. Over time, Stitch Fix's algorithms analyze customer feedback, style ratings, Pinterest boards, and even weather patterns to refine its recommendations.

Generative AI goes even further, creating personalized outfit suggestions that fit the customer's profile and anticipate future preferences based on trends and behavioral data.

However, the magic happens when human stylists step in to fine-tune these recommendations. By blending the efficiency of AI with the creativity, empathy, and intuition of human stylists, Stitch Fix elevates every customer interaction to a truly exceptional MX and CX.

For example, while AI might recommend a floral blouse based on data patterns, a stylist could notice that a customer has an upcoming event and suggest pairing the blouse with a tailored skirt for a polished look. The stylist then includes a personal note explaining the customer's choices and offering styling tips. These notes go beyond marketing clothes—they create a sense of collaboration, reinforcing the *Power of We* by making customers feel valued and understood.

This hybrid approach also allows Stitch Fix to handle unique customer needs that AI alone might miss. Whether it's avoiding certain fabrics for sensitive skin or tailoring selections for a client's lifestyle changes, human stylists ensure that every Fix feels deeply personal.

But the benefits don't stop there. Human stylists provide qualitative feedback to Stitch Fix's algorithms, helping the AI learn and improve over time. This ongoing feedback loop blends technology's scalability with human intelligence's artistry, ensuring that the personalization process improves with each customer interaction. I can personally attest that the fashion picks are accurate, from the sizing to the fit to the style preferences. Over several years, I did not receive one item that wasn't *me*.

Why does this matter? *Because fashion is emotional.* Customers aren't just looking for clothes; they're looking for confidence, comfort, and style for specific moments in their lives. While AI excels at recognizing patterns, only humans can understand the emotional nuances that drive a customer's choices. By combining these strengths, Stitch Fix creates a shopping experience that resonates on both a practical and emotional level.

Even with the challenges of a competitive market, Stitch Fix's AI-driven strategy positions it as a brand that understands its fans better than they sometimes understand themselves. **The company has shown that fan-centric marketing isn't just about knowing your audience—it's about anticipating their needs before they even voice them.** We learn from the Stitch Fix case study that personalization builds trust, loyalty, and, ultimately, superfans.

Stitch Fix's marketing is just as powerful as its technology. Its "Personal Styling for Everybody" tagline underscores an inclusive, fan-focused approach. Stitch Fix doesn't market itself as an elite service for fashionistas; instead, it champions the idea that everyone—regardless of size, age, or budget—deserves to feel confident and stylish. For example, one of their broadcast TV commercials echoes this sentiment: "We don't just see your size or style. We see YOU."

The graphics, photos, and copy used in Stitch Fix's marketing convey that Stitch Fix is about YOU, the fan, not about them. You'll notice the marketing doesn't focus on the super cute clothes they sell, the expertise of their stylists, the number of customers they have obtained, their rapid growth, the multi-billion-dollar valuation, or the fantastic AI behind their stylist picks. Those groundbreaking achievements are undoubtedly laudable, and it would be easy and tempting to make them the focus of the marketing message. What if the tagline and message were "Styled by The Best," "Styled for Rock Stars by Rock Stars," or "Groundbreaking Style at Your Service." The problem with these fictional taglines is that they are about the brand, not the fan.

Your fans have zero tolerance for irrelevant marketing campaigns and canned sales pitches.

Is your marketing about you, the brand, or about your FANS? This book is titled FANtastic Marketing because the marketing that converts shoppers into buyers and prospects into clients is *for* the fans, *about* the fans, and ultimately generated *by* the fans. The FAN comes first with FANtastic Marketing—quite literally—it's the beginning of the word.

YOUR FANS EXPECT PERSONALIZATION

The Stitch Fix model exemplifies how businesses can harness the power of AI to deepen their connection with fans. It's a fan-centric marketing approach designed *for the fans* and *all about the fans*.

Your fans don't have the time or patience for anything that doesn't pertain directly to them. Yet, they're willing to pay a premium for someone to organize and curate their choices. Today, personalization and customization are not just preferences—they're expectations. Tools powered by artificial intelligence (AI) make it possible to deliver this level of personalization at scale, creating unique experiences for every fan without losing efficiency.

Consider these paradigm shifts:

- What if you started treating your clients, customers, buyers, prospects, guests, ups, leads, and online followers like FANS at a rock concert or sports event?
- What if you started calling prospective customers FANS instead of cold terms like ups, prospects, or leads that imply no relationship?
- What if your marketing gave your FANS precisely what they want when they want it?
- And what if your FANS became the focus of your marketing campaigns?

By making these shifts, you will build greater brand awareness, increase engagement, drive traffic, and, most importantly, close more sales. Tools like AI-powered analytics and personalization engines help you scale these efforts, ensuring your strategies resonate deeply with your audience and amplify the power of The Fan Factor by identifying superfans, analyzing their behaviors, and delivering hyper-targeted campaigns that turn satisfied customers into brand advocates.

THE FAN FACTOR™

Once your fans become engaged, loyal, and utterly rabid about your brand, they start doing the selling and marketing for you. I call this *The Fan Factor.*

The Fan Factor happens when your fans:

- Post rave reviews about your product or service online.
- Refer others through word of mouth or social media shoutouts.
- Use your tagline or brand message to describe your business positively.
- Use your product name as a noun or a verb to describe the entire product category, like Kleenex® or FedEx®.

The good news is you don't have to be a large company like Stitch Fix or Progressive to implement these strategies. Small business owners and entrepreneurs can harness the principles of fan-centric marketing and incorporate AI tools on a smaller scale to achieve significant results. Affordable AI-powered platforms like Mailchimp®, Canva®, or ChatGPT by Open AI allow businesses of any size to deliver personalized marketing, manage customer relationships, and engage fans effectively. It's not about how big your budget is—it's about how intentional and fan-focused your strategy can be.

In the modern sales environment, the only way to gain new customers and retain existing customers is to utilize The Fan Factor. The Fan Factor operates differently than the conventional direct sales pitch. With the traditional approach, the more you try to sell and market directly to your target audience, the more it tunes you out. It's like at the dinner table when you are trying to get your child to eat broccoli. The more Mom or Dad tries to convince, threaten, and punish the child to eat broccoli, the more the child resists. But as soon as a friend comes over and declares an undying love for broccoli, suddenly, the kid loves it too and gobbles it down. Getting your child to eat vegetables (or whatever they don't like at the dinner table) is the ultimate example of The Fan Factor at work.

WHY FANTASTIC MARKETING?

BECAUSE TOO OFTEN, your fans can't hear you.

Consider the amount of advertising aimed at customers these days. Approximately PER SECOND:[4]

- **X® tweets sent:** 9,000
- **Instagram® photos uploaded:** 1,000
- **TikToks® uploaded:** 273[5]
- **Google® searches conducted:** 80,000
- **YouTube® videos viewed:** 82,000
- **Emails sent:** Nearly 2.9 million
- **Zoom® meetings started:** 69

And that's just online activity. What about the offline marketing and sales messages that inundate us daily, from bumper stickers to billboards, radio commercials to direct mail, and print ads to point-of-sale displays? Today's consumers are deafened by a cacophony of marketing information that sounds like Charlie Brown's teacher giving instructions for a pop quiz. The sheer volume of messaging has created an environment where consumers are overwhelmed and tuning out.

What does this mean for your business?

It means your customers are *connected* more than ever, but they're also more *distracted* than ever.

If you want to break through the noise, you can't rely on the old "look at my brand" approach. Instead, you need a strategy that cuts through the chaos by focusing on what your fans genuinely care about.

WE HAVE POPCORN BRAIN AND BRAIN ROT

We spend so much of our waking hours consuming media, primarily online, because it feeds our brains the instant gratification, speed, and unpredictability we crave. Some of us are so hooked we neglect offline tasks and relationships in favor of being online. If this sounds geeky, pathetic, or unreasonable, don't be so quick to judge.

Answer these questions honestly:

- Have you ever felt compelled to check your email at a completely inappropriate time, just in case something important has come in?
- Have you ever forgotten or lost your phone and felt panicked until it was located?
- How often is your phone further than arm's length away from you at any point during the day and night?

- How many computers, phones, tablets, and televisions do you own? Are there as many devices as people in your household, or perhaps even more?

- How many streaming apps like Netflix® or Apple TV® do you subscribe to? Do you frequently forget where to find what streaming show to watch because you have so many apps that it's hard to remember?

- Do you have to listen to music, news, audiobooks, or podcasts while you work, exercise, or clean the house because silence feels awkward and depressing?

Researcher David Levy calls this phenomenon "popcorn brain," defined as a brain so accustomed to the constant stimulation of electronic multitasking that its owner soon becomes unfit for life offline, where events transpire at a much slower pace. In this day and age, we all suffer from a bit of popcorn brain, and this tendency isn't a personality flaw but rather a biological imperative. Why? It's because the human brain craves stimulation and new information.

The 2024 Word of the Year by Oxford University Press (OUP) is brain rot.[6] I know that is technically two words, but *hey*, I don't make the rules for OUP. The language specialists at OUP compiled a six-word shortlist that captures the moods and discussions that influenced the past year. Following two weeks of public voting and extensive dialogue, the experts convened to review the public feedback, voting outcomes, and linguistic data. **OUP found the use of brain rot increased in frequency by 230% between 2023 and 2024.**

Brain rot is defined by OUP as "the supposed deterioration of a person's mental or intellectual state, especially viewed as the result of overconsumption of material (now particularly online content) considered to be trivial or unchallenging."

One of the most common mistakes marketers make is thinking that a lack of response equals a lack of interest. This is not true. Your fans are distracted with popcorn brain and brain rot. It's a wonder we marketers get any degree of their attention! It's your job to speak clearly and connect with them on an emotional level so that they can and will pay attention to your message.

A lack of *engagement* does not necessarily equal a lack of *interest*.

Please note that if your business has a negative reputation for poor customer experience, you cannot blame popcorn brain and brain rot. Refocus your efforts on creating a wow experience for your customers. Once you have a tribe of satisfied, raving fans, return to this book. **No amount of FANtastic Marketing can overcome a bad reputation.**

If you have raving fans who are not engaging, I promise you it is because the marketing message is not about them. Is your sales and marketing message so compelling, engaging, informative, and credible that it's worth dropping everything to listen to? It will be if it is about the fans and for the fans!

TODAY'S CONSUMERS TAKE MULTITASKING TO A WHOLE NEW LEVEL

Not only do consumers spend significant time interacting with media, but most of us also pay attention to more than one media source at a time. Researchers call this *media multitasking*. Today, people go to sleep and wake up with the phone within reach while simultaneously streaming music, turning on the muted television to a cable news channel, checking email, scanning their Facebook or X feed, and then texting a few friends (and all this before shower and coffee). More than **90%** of smartphone users check their mobile devices within the first hour of getting up.[7] Most of us even media multitask in the bathroom!

Wikipedia® defines media multitasking this way:

> *Using TV, the web, radio, telephone, print, or any other media in conjunction with another. Also referred to as 'simultaneous media use,' this behavior has emerged as increasingly common, especially among younger media users, and has gained significant attention in media usage measurement, especially as a new opportunity for cross-media advertising.*[8]

In the US, on average, **smartphone users touch their devices 2,617 times a day**! Most individuals use their phone for **more than four hours daily**, with **11%** saying they use it for **more than seven hours daily**. Only 5% of Americans said they use their phones for less than an hour a day.[9]

If this sounds like you, you are a media multitasker. It's not that you don't want to pay attention (in most cases). Instead, you multitask. You feel compelled to do so because you have popcorn brain, and there's so much information available that you have little choice but to spread your attention among several media sources and hope something sinks in.

The ability to focus on one task at a time has been fundamentally altered by the daily realities of modern life. A Boston College study on media multitasking found that participants placed in a room with a television and a computer, given a half hour to use either device, **switched their gaze between the two screens an average of 120 times in just 27.5 minutes—almost once every 14 seconds.**[10] The multitaskers who believed they could successfully split their attention between a TV show and the information on their computer screens were mistaken. The concurrent use of the two devices led to overwhelming distraction. This explains why many parents insist on doing homework without distractions from YouTube or TikTok.

Given how distracted fans are you have two options:

☛ **Option 1—Fight for attention.**

In this strategy, the business owner stakes out a space in the marketplace and broadcasts their message loudly and frequently enough to be noticed and heard. This strategy is known as Outbound Marketing. There are certainly use cases for Outbound Marketing (OM). However, remember that competing for attention demands a substantial budget because we use more expensive marketing tactics, such as broadcast television commercials, product placements in streaming shows, celebrity endorsements, and extravagant events. Fighting for attention is not feasible for many entrepreneurs and small businesses.

Are you willing and prepared to make this significant financial commitment investment?

☛ **Option 2—Ask for as little attention as possible.**

What? Have I lost my mind? Not a chance! *Here's the big news:* with this option, the business owner **calmly and elegantly attracts consumers** instead of battling for market share because the message is *about* and *for* them. This is called Inbound Marketing (IM). By using this approach, business owners, entrepreneurs, and influencers facilitate easy engagement for fans by positioning themselves in a digital space where one click suffices, no matter how distracted the customer might be.

This option may seem counterintuitive since most sales and marketing leaders are trained and encouraged to dominate the conversation, discuss the brand, and capture the client's attention for as long as possible. However, the business owner who can let go of outdated thinking and embrace The Fan Factor possesses a unique magic, drawing customers like iron filings to a magnet. The result? A flourishing crowd of fans significantly boosting sales.

FANS ARE THE ANSWER

In this attention-starved world, your fans hold the key to success. Make your marketing all about your fans. Instead of trying to dominate the conversation, focus on their desires, interests, and aspirations. When you align your messaging with their needs, they'll stop scrolling and start listening.

Don't try to outshout the competition or outspend big brands. Do the opposite. Whisper.

Thanks to technological advances, even small businesses can cut through the noise. AI tools allow you to analyze customer behavior, predict what your fans want, and deliver the perfect message at the perfect time. Whether it's a personalized email campaign, a chatbot that feels like a conversation, or social media ads tailored to individual preferences, AI makes it possible to engage distracted customers with precision and impact.

Part II

THE PLAYERS

"For a team to be motivated enough to win, each individual member must be motivated."

Tom Landry, Hall of Fame NFL Coach of the Dallas Cowboys, 1960 – 1988

OUR SUPERFAN CULTURE

WHY DO I USE the fan analogy? **Because we live in a superfan culture!** There's a community for every passion, from car enthusiasts to devoted bookworms and binge-worthy TV show followers. The Anchorage Museum in Anchorage, AL, has even hosted an art museum exhibition on fandom, celebrating various forms of fandom, from movies to music, television to comic books.[11] In 2018, I had the opportunity to visit the *Art of Fandom* exhibit. It was FANtastic; I took so many pictures!

Beyond museum exhibitions, in today's hyper-connected world, online platforms like Reddit®, Discord®, and TikTok make it easier than ever for superfans to connect, engage deeply, and amplify their shared interests.

THE REDDIT REVOLUTION

If you're looking for proof of how superfans unite, look no further than Reddit. With over **57 million daily active users** and more than **100,000 active communities (subreddits)**, Reddit is the go-to platform for superfans to discuss, debate, and celebrate everything from the latest TV show cliffhangers to niche hobbies like restoring vintage cameras.[12] Subreddits such as **r/books**, **r/television**, and **r/MarvelStudios** flourish as passionate hubs where fans dissect plotlines, share theories, and build excitement for upcoming releases.

What makes Reddit a standout platform for superfans? **It has a sense of authenticity and grassroots engagement.** Reddit prioritizes in-depth discussions, user-generated content, and real-time fan reactions. The platform thrives on upvotes, downvotes, and comments that make superfans feel seen and heard.

For example, when a TV series like *The Last of Us* airs, fans flock to subreddits like **r/TheLastOfUs** to analyze each episode, share Easter eggs, and post memes. Studios and brands often monitor these conversations to gauge audience sentiment and tweak their marketing strategies based on fan feedback. In this way, Reddit isn't just a platform for superfans—it's a research and development goldmine for brands to understand their most passionate audiences and create innovative MX and products/services in high demand by fans.

THE NEW ERA OF SUPERFAN PLATFORMS

Reddit isn't alone in cultivating superfandom. Platforms like **Discord** allow fans to build private servers to chat in real time, host watch parties, and share exclusive content. Meanwhile, **TikTok's algorithm** takes superfandom viral by serving users hyper-personalized content based on their interests. From #BookTok recommendations that sell out entire book series to fan-made trailers for upcoming movies, TikTok turns superfandom into a cultural movement.

Please note: does this mean your business needs to start a Discord channel or a TikTok account immediately? Maybe. Throughout the book, I will provide many examples, tactics, channels, and tools. However, that does **NOT** mean that all of them are suitable for your business. So, don't assume I am endorsing it for everyone just because I mention something. The tactics, tools, and channels to use depend on who your fans are—and we will cover this in-depth in Secrets #3 and #5.

WHAT THIS MEANS FOR YOUR MARKETING

The superfan tendency is why people will pay a premium for a Starbucks® latte or wait in line overnight for the latest iPhone®. It is why fans spend hours painting their faces and donning elaborate costumes to cheer for their team on game day. Humans are hardwired to connect and commit to our passions. Let's face it: we are passionate people who like to commit to our passions wholeheartedly.

Are you tapping into that need with your marketing? If not, now is the time. Platforms like Reddit and TikTok show superfans are more engaged than ever.

By creating spaces where your fans connect, share, and celebrate your brand, you're not just marketing—you're building a *movement*.

VOTERS ARE FANS TOO

Before we explore how FANtastic Marketing is utilized in presidential campaigns to attract voters, I acknowledge that discussing politics can be partisan and divisive. In today's climate, political conversations often evoke strong emotions, which is completely understandable. **However, as marketers, we must strive to remain objective.** I hope you never find yourself marketing a product or service you oppose. But if you do, examining the marketing of a candidate you did not vote for will prepare you. I promise to highlight both red and blue campaigns. The discussion will be objective and even across party platforms.

We have a unique opportunity to analyze arguably the most well-known, high-stakes, and big-budget marketing campaign in the world: the presidential election for the leader of the free world. These campaigns are significant case studies in branding, budgeting, marketing strategies, fan engagement, emotional resonance, and innovative technologies like AI.

Let's dive in—**not as voters, but as marketers**—eager to learn from some of history's most innovative, expensive, and impactful marketing campaigns.

TURN OUT THE BASE

In the political world, fans are referred to as the base. The **2004 Bush-Cheney** campaign was the first to demonstrate how robust an engaged fan "base" can be on Election Day. Before the 2004 election, the predominant political strategy focused on **swing voters**, defined by Wikipedia as "a voter who may not be affiliated with a particular political party (Independent) or not vote across party lines."[13]

In the PBS television special, *Karl Rove—The Architect*, Chief Campaign Strategist for Bush-Cheney 2004, Matthew O'Dowd talks about a critical decision made by the Bush campaign. Instead of focusing on independent swing voters, the Bush campaign emphasized **mobilizing the base of Republican voters (aka the fans)** known as the Compassionate Conservatives. O'Dowd looked at the voter turnout from the 2000 election and discovered the following.

> "...Independents or persuadable voters in the last 20 years had gone from 22% of the electorate to 7% of the electorate in 2000. And so we concluded that...93 or 94% in 2004...was already going to be decided either for us or against us. You obviously had to do fairly well among the 6 or 7%, but you could lose the 6 or 7% and win the election, which was fairly revolutionary because everybody up until that time had said, 'Swing voters, swing voters, swing voters, swing voters, swing voters.'"[14]

By the 2020 Presidential election, both major US campaigns demonstrated the importance of *engaging their base* while leveraging technology. The **Biden-Harris** campaign, for instance, used **predictive analytics and AI-powered tools** to identify voter behavior, refine messaging, and predict turnout. They targeted younger voters through text campaigns and TikTok ads while connecting with older demographics via personalized emails.

Similarly, the **2020 Trump-Pence** campaign leveraged **AI psychographics** to create micro-targeted ads on Facebook and Instagram. These ads analyzed user data to pinpoint personality traits, allowing the campaign to deliver highly personalized content that resonated emotionally.

THE YOUTUBE PRESIDENT

The **2008 Obama-Biden** ticket was the **first presidential campaign to harness the power of the Internet and Social Media to engage the base.** Both candidates used the Internet to reach voters. However, Team Obama mastered the medium and the message of *Hope and Change* early and exploited it to the hilt. Along the way, it changed politics—and government—perhaps forever.[15]

The Obama-Biden campaign went to great lengths to maximize its social media engagement. What made the Obama-Biden campaign so effective? **First, they created a social network of both new and highly energized long-time fans.** In political terms, they established an *online base* of followers. Second, they consistently provided fans with **highly targeted, personalized online content**, including:

- Text messages for younger voters
- Email campaigns for older voters
- Online ads targeted based on browsing history
- YouTube videos
- Blog posts
- Online contests for donors

Fast-forward four years to 2012. Obama-Biden is seeking a second term, and they are competing against Mitt Romney and Paul Ryan. The **2012 Romney-Ryan** campaign was more effective on social media than were previous Republican candidates (particularly with conservative women voters) but still fell short compared to the 2012 Obama-Biden campaign. You may remember one of the main issues of the 2012 campaign was the "Republican War on Women." In response to that accusation, the Romney-Ryan campaign quickly published a Facebook page for *Moms for Mitt*. The page attracted more than 70,000 fans in four days, which was notable then, considering this was before the widespread usage of sponsored posts and paid ads on Facebook.

THE UNEXPECTED WINNER OF 2016 AND 2024

It's fair to say that almost no one anticipated the 2016 election results. Nearly every professional pollster predicted an easy **Clinton-Kaine** victory that year. However, if we take a step back and examine both the Trump-Pence and Clinton-Kaine campaigns through the lens of FANtastic Marketing, the outcome we witnessed at 2 a.m. on November 9, 2016, is as obvious as counting on Tom Brady to win seven Super Bowl titles.

Love him or loathe him, objectively speaking, Donald Trump is a master marketer.

If you dislike his personality or his presidency, please don't stop reading. While many debate his style and substance, we can't dispute the results from 2016 and 2024, which are now recorded in the annals of history. Continue reading if you want to stay at the top of your marketing game and learn from the failures and victories of others.

MAGA® UNLEASHED

The success of the Make America Great Again (MAGA) movement wasn't accidental; it was built on a strategic foundation that leveraged audience insights, clear messaging, and innovative communication channels. Let's break down the key steps that fueled its impact, starting with identifying a neglected audience.

Step #1—Identified a Neglected Audience

In 2016, Donald Trump recognized a target audience long overlooked by traditional politicians, now called "The Forgotten Men and Women." These voters felt alienated and disenfranchised, many participating in the political process for the first time. Trump emerged as the central figure this group could rally around, giving them a sense of belonging and validation.

This same strategy continued into the 2020 campaign but with a significant difference: the enthusiasm that fueled the 2016 victory began to wane among specific base segments. Political analysts have pointed out that while Trump successfully maintained his core group of superfans, some previously energized voters did not turn out in 2020, contributing to Joe Biden's victory. **The lesson here is clear for businesses and marketers: engaging new customers is critical, but retaining and re-energizing existing fans is just as important.**

Step #2—Crafted a Clear and Memorable Message

Trump's 2016 campaign slogan, "Make America Great Again," resonated deeply because it connected with his target audience's emotional fears and aspirations. The message focused on the fans—highlighting their concerns about the southern border, the economy, cultural changes, and perceived neglect by political elites. It was straightforward, memorable, and easy to repeat.

In contrast, the 2020 campaign sought to build on the MAGA brand with the slogan "Keep America Great." While this appealed to core supporters, it did not energize new audiences as effectively as MAGA did in 2016. Meanwhile, Joe Biden's 2020 slogan, "Build Back Better," resonated with voters looking for unity and recovery after years of political turmoil and the COVID-19 pandemic.

The takeaway for marketers is that **messaging must evolve to address current circumstances while maintaining an emotional connection** that resonates with your audience. Stale or overly familiar messaging can fall flat, even with a loyal fan base.

Step #3—Leveraged Key Channels

Trump's ability to communicate directly with his audience remained a cornerstone of his campaigns in 2016 and 2020. In 2016, Trump mastered social media to bypass legacy media, connecting directly with his supporters and controlling the narrative. The in-person rallies also played a crucial role in generating energy, fostering a sense of community, and amplifying his message.

By 2020, however, Trump's reliance on social media began to yield diminishing returns. The changing algorithms of the platforms and increasing polarization meant his messaging often reached the same core audience instead of expanding to new voters.[16]

At the same time, Biden's campaign relied heavily on a broader digital strategy, utilizing **AI-driven ad targeting**, **social listening tools**, and **platforms like TikTok** to engage younger voters and diverse demographics. Biden's use of data analytics enabled his campaign to deploy highly targeted messages, ensuring maximum engagement with specific voter groups.

Biden's victory came down to two key factors:

1. **Broadening the Coalition**—Biden's campaign successfully expanded its appeal to independents, suburban voters[17], and traditionally Republican demographics, such as older Americans concerned about Trump's handling of the pandemic.[18]

2. **Turnout and Engagement**—While Trump energized a portion of his base, the Biden-Harris campaign benefited from record-breaking voter turnout, particularly among young voters and communities of color. This success was largely due to their data-driven approach, which included micro-targeted outreach and AI-enhanced voter engagement strategies.[19]

For marketers, this illustrates the importance of retaining loyal customers and continuously growing your audience by addressing their specific needs and concerns.

Step #4—Lessons from Trump's Presidential Campaigns

What can marketers learn from Trump's campaigns? A few key takeaways include:

- **Create Emotional Resonance**—Trump's slogans—whether MAGA or Keep America Great—worked because they addressed deep emotional concerns. Marketers should aim to craft messages that tap into their audience's fears, hopes, or aspirations.

- **Evolve Your Channels**—While Trump thrived on social media in 2016, Biden's use of AI, TikTok, and other platforms highlighted the need to meet audiences where they are. Staying updated on emerging trends and tools is critical for sustained success.

- **Sustain Momentum**—Trump's declining turnout in 2020 highlights the risk of taking core fans for granted. Brands and campaigns must actively re-engage their base while expanding their reach.

MOVING FORWARD

Imagine your business as a political campaign. Would your supporters believe so passionately that "every vote counts" that they would wait in line for hours, even in bad weather? Are you inspiring your fans to show up when it matters most? Does your messaging address the emotional needs of your audience? Are you using the latest tools—like AI, social media, and data-driven insights—to keep your fans engaged and growing?

Set a goal to reenergize your base while broadening your reach. As the 2020 election demonstrated, sustained engagement with existing and new audiences is essential to winning, whether it's a campaign or customer loyalty.

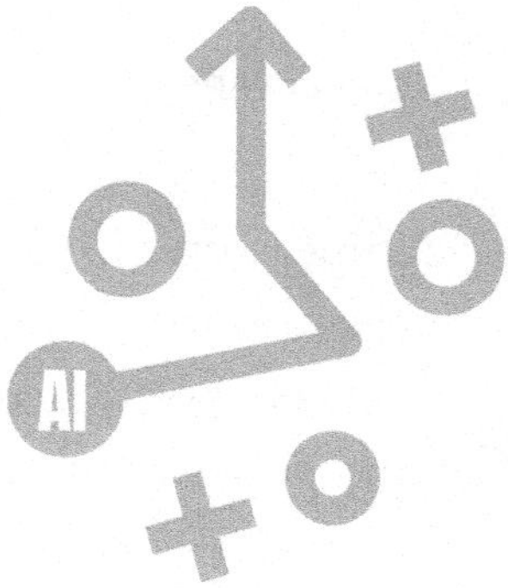

THE DNA OF A FAN

TRANSITIONING FROM THE REALM of political campaigns, where we examined fans as collective groups rallying around shared causes, we now turn our attention to sports fans to uncover the **psychology of individual fandom**. Political campaigns illustrate how fans unite to achieve a common goal.

Sports fandom provides a more intimate lens, revealing how deeply personal connections to a team or athlete shapes behavior, identity, and loyalty.

If you aren't into sports, take a moment to reflect on what hobby, passion, or cause you are entirely devoted to. The DNA traits discussed in this section apply to any fandom—from gardening to gaming, shopping to skiing, comic books to concerts.

To truly understand the psychology of fandom, marketers must delve deeper into what drives their audience on an individual level. Why does a die-hard sports fan paint their face, endure freezing temperatures to attend a game, or religiously follow a team even in seasons of crushing losses? What inspires someone to remain loyal to their favorite brand, product, or influencer in the same way? The answer lies in the **DNA of a fan**—five crucial traits that marketers can utilize to turn casual customers into dedicated superfans.

Bleacherreport.com[20] outlines the following five reasons for extreme sports fan behavior:

DNA TRAIT #1—IDENTITY

A fan's devotion begins with a **shared identity**. For many, being a fan of a team or brand is more than a preference—it's a core part of who they are. A fan doesn't just cheer for their team; they say, "**I am** a Lakers fan," "**I am** a Patriots fan," or "**I am** a Taylor Swift's Swiftie." This identity shapes how they see themselves and how others see them.

"Our sports heroes are our warriors," says Robert Cialdini, a professor of psychology at Arizona State. Cialdini explains, "This is not some **light diversion** to be enjoyed for its inherent grace and harmony. The **self is centrally involved** in the event's outcome."[21]

I know Cialdini's observation is accurate from watching my dad and husband. According to my dad—though my mom disagrees—I was named after Dandy Don Meredith, an award-winning quarterback for the Dallas Cowboys. My dad's sports fandom influenced my name! Growing up, when my dad was a pastor, it was widely known among the church that if the Florida Gators won on Saturday, we could expect him to wear a Gator necktie in the pulpit for Sunday's sermon. It made the Florida State Seminole church members mad! LOL!

I had been married for about 10 years when I first started studying uber sports fandom. I needed to understand better why my husband wore Miami Hurricanes licensed logo apparel. Every. Single. Day! I'm not kidding or exaggerating for effect. And guess what—more than 15 years later, he is still wearing it, EVERY. SINGLE. DAY. SMH!

Rabid sports fans experience the results of their cherished sports events so personally; it's as if they're catching the game-winning touchdown on the field. Fans often say, "**WE** won the game!" or "**WE** need to fire the coach!" Even though "**WE**" aren't part of the team! SuperFans feel like the 12th player, ready to jump in and substitute at a moment's notice! It's truly the *Power of We* at work!

Ask any fan why they follow a particular team; the answer usually indicates this deep emotional identification. They'll usually say something like, "I don't know - I just always have," or "My grandad always roots for this team. I've been following them my whole life." As you can see, the connection is sometimes passed on through the generations.

The sense of identity a fan feels is a result of a personal or shared connection.

Sometimes, a shared connection arises from geography. My strong family roots in a small town near Gainesville, FL, along with many family members who are alumni—including my dad and brother—mean that I have always been and will always be a Florida Gator fan. *It's simply part of who I am.*

I was fortunate to receive a full scholarship to the University of Central Florida (UCF) in Orlando, so I did not attend the University of Florida® (UF). At that time, UCF lacked an on-campus stadium and a competitive football team, so most students—myself included—supported another football team. Go Gators!

If you aren't a sports fan, I want to ensure you can still IDENTIFY (see what I did there) with this point. There are so many examples of passions and hobbies that create a shared identity—here are a few that might resonate with you more than the sports analogy.

- **Music and Concerts**—music festivals, concerts, or joining fan clubs for specific artists or bands (e.g., BTS Army, Deadheads) creates a solid shared identity among fans.

- **Cultural or Religious Gatherings**—participating in cultural festivals, religious ceremonies, or faith-based groups brings people together through shared traditions, values, and beliefs.

- **Gaming Communities**—online multiplayer games (e.g., Fortnite®, World of Warcraft®) and gaming conventions provide a shared identity for gamers who collaborate, compete, and bond over their favorite titles.

- **Fandoms and Pop Culture**—fandoms for TV shows, movies, or book series (e.g., Star Wars®, Harry Potter®, Marvel®) create communities that share a love for fictional worlds and characters.

- **Volunteering or Activism**—being part of volunteer groups or activism movements (e.g., environmental advocacy, LGBTQ+

rights, humanitarian aid) fosters a shared sense of purpose and identity by making an impact.

- **Creative Communities**—artistic groups, like theater troupes, writing workshops, or photography clubs, allow people to express themselves while bonding over shared passions.

- **Social Media Groups and Forums**—engaging in online communities like Reddit subreddits, Facebook Groups, or Discord servers for niche interests provides a shared identity and a connection around hobbies or causes.

- **Educational or Professional Groups**—being part of alumni associations, study groups, or professional organizations connects people through shared goals, values, and experiences in education or work. For me, membership in the National Association of Home Builders and National Speakers Association has profoundly impacted my career by contributing to my knowledge and skills. Most importantly, I've been fortunate to develop lifelong friendships that mean more than any professional achievement.

- **Fitness Groups**—group workouts, running clubs, or yoga retreats offer camaraderie and identity around shared wellness goals.

- **Food and Wine Enthusiasts**—joining cooking classes, wine tastings, or foodie tours brings people together over shared interests in culinary experiences.

- **Political or Civic Engagement**—involvement in political parties, civic action groups, or campaign efforts provides identity and belonging through shared ideologies or goals for societal change.

- **Parenting or Support Groups**—parents often form strong connections through playgroups, school organizations, or online communities like "mom blogs" or "dad networks."

- **Outdoor Activities**—groups focused on hiking, camping, or bird-watching build a shared identity among those who love nature and the outdoors.

- **Maker Communities**—DIY enthusiasts, tech hobbyists, and builders (e.g., 3D printing enthusiasts and LEGO® fans) bond through their love of creating and innovating.

Each activity or group represents a unique way to cultivate a shared identity, and marketers can tap into these communities by aligning campaigns with their values, symbols, and passions.

AI and Digitally Shared Identities

In today's digital age, **AI has revolutionized how fans connect with and express their identities.** AI-driven platforms and tools empower individuals to see themselves reflected in the brands, communities, and content they love.

- **Personalized Experiences**—Tools like Spotify® Wrapped and Audible® use AI to curate unique year-end summaries that celebrate users' listening habits and encourage them to embrace and share their musical identities.

- **Gaming and Virtual Identities**—AI-powered customization in games like The Sims™ and Fortnite allows fans to create characters that reflect their authentic or aspirational selves, turning virtual worlds into spaces for self-expression.

- **AI-Generated Avatars**—Apps like Lensa® AI enable fans to design digital avatars that align with their personalities, blending technology with creativity to enhance self-expression.

Nike's® app uses AI to recommend workout plans and gear based on user activity, reinforcing users' identities as athletes or fitness enthusiasts. Social listening tools like Brandwatch® analyze online conversations to uncover cultural movements and niche communities. By aligning with identity groups such as eco-conscious consumers or gaming enthusiasts, brands can tailor their messaging to reflect their fans' values and lifestyles authentically.

These AI-driven experiences show fans that brands genuinely understand who they are and what they stand for, reinforcing loyalty and deepening emotional connections.

How Well Do You Know Your Fans?

Few brands understand the power of identity like Anheuser-Busch®. Their iconic Clydesdale commercials widely evoke feelings of nostalgia, unity, and pride, striking a chord with audiences across generations. These ads, often tied to major events like the Super Bowl® or national holidays, tell deeply emotional stories that resonate universally. Whether it's a heartwarming tale of perseverance, a nod to tradition, or a tribute to togetherness, these commercials leverage the emotional connection between the brand and its fans, creating memorable and shareable moments.

To fully understand the concept of identity, ask yourself or a passionate sports fan these questions:

- What elevated the chosen team or sports figure over all other teams or sports figures to claim extreme loyalty?
- When or how did the interest start? Why do fans remain avidly interested?

THE BALL IS IN YOUR COURT—PRACTICE DRILL #1

Consumers know when a brand connects to The *Power of We* and when it misses the mark. The next time you find yourself scratching your head at a television/streaming ad that doesn't make sense, think about why not. Was it the graphics, use of or lack of humor, the actors, or the message? Regardless of what aspect missed the mark, I guarantee it didn't appeal to you because it failed to make an emotional connection.

Takeaway for Marketers: Does your brand connect with your audience's sense of identity? Are you helping them say, "This is who I am and what I stand for."

DNA TRAIT #2—SELF-ESTEEM

Because sports fans strongly identify with their teams or favorite players, their self-esteem can fluctuate with the success of those teams or individuals. Psychologist Dr. Daniel Wann's research on enthusiastic sports fans found that a *deep interest in a team can protect people from depression and promote feelings of self-worth.*[22]

Conversely, researchers have also discovered that fans who experience a loss by their team feel less optimistic about their lives, whether it involves asking someone out, excelling at work, or winning a game of darts. For sports fans, players are heroes who personify bravery, discipline, and resilience—qualities that motivate fans to strive harder and enhance their self-esteem. However, the connection works both ways: when a fan's hero stumbles, the fan feels that loss intensely, often questioning their inner strength.

Fans also love an underdog story. Witnessing an underdog triumph against all odds creates a powerful "If they can do it, so can I" effect. Brands that harness this emotional uplift can deeply connect with consumers. Unfortunately, the opposite is often true: fans frequently feel their dreams are threatened when a cherished hero or brand falters.

Your fans want to feel good about themselves, and your brand, product, or service can be part of that equation.

The iconic L'Oréal® tagline, "Because I'm Worth It," is a FANtastic example of marketing self-esteem. Written in 1973, this timeless phrase became synonymous with the brand, conveying empowerment and self-worth to women everywhere. To this day, L'Oréal continues to use the tagline, which still resonates with fans because it appeals to self-esteem. According to L'Oréal's research, 80% of women recognize and respond to this positive, aspirational message.[23]

A contemporary example of self-esteem marketing can be found in TikTok's algorithms, which empower users by curating personalized content that aligns with their interests and passions. Whether it's discovering new fitness tips, personal finance hacks, or relatable mental health advice, TikTok's AI-driven content feels like a boost of confidence tailored just for you. This deeply personalized approach helps users feel seen and capable, reinforcing their self-worth.

Pinterest®—A Platform for Aspiration

Another shining example is Pinterest, a platform that thrives on aspiration and personal growth. **As of 2023, Pinterest has over 450 million monthly active users, 60% of whom identify as women.**[24] The platform's appeal lies in its ability to help users visualize their goals and take actionable steps toward achieving them.

Pinterest inspires users to improve their lives with a wealth of how-to content tailored to their interests, whether meal prepping, interior decorating, or mastering the latest fitness routine. The site's design makes self-improvement accessible, giving users the confidence to tackle any project or goal with a step-by-step guide. Brands that excel on Pinterest understand their fans' aspirations and provide empowering content that supports them.

For marketers, platforms like Pinterest and TikTok provide a blueprint for empowering fans. By helping fans visualize success and achieve their personal goals, brands foster deeper emotional connections that translate to loyalty.

The Role of AI in Self-Esteem Marketing

In the digital age, AI-driven tools play a significant role in shaping self-esteem marketing. Here's how:

1. **Personalization**—AI allows brands to create hyper-specific, confidence-boosting content tailored to individual users' preferences. Platforms like Instagram and Spotify use AI to suggest playlists, workouts, or activities that align with users' aspirations, enhancing their sense of control and achievement.

2. **Augmented Reality (AR)**—Brands like Sephora® and Warby Parker empower fans with AR tools that let them "try on" products virtually. This builds self-esteem by giving users confidence in their choices, creating FANS before they buy, and enhancing the MX.

3. **Chatbots for Encouragement**—As discussed with the Progressive Insurance Flo Chatbot, AI-powered chatbots are evolving beyond customer service to provide encouragement and motivation. For example, fitness apps like Noom® use chatbots to celebrate milestones and motivate users.

Empowering Your Fans

In today's feel-good society, brands that empower consumers win big. It's not just about selling a product or service—it's about helping your fans feel good about themselves.

How does your product or service contribute to your customers' confidence, goals, or self-worth? More importantly, how do your interactions with fans reflect this empowerment?

Ask yourself:

- How do you feel when your favorite team wins or when you see your music idol in concert? How does that affect your outlook on life?
- On the other hand, how do you feel when they lose or fall from grace? How does that emotional dip impact your day or week?
- If you're not a sports fan, consider your hobby or passion. When you participate in it, does it boost your confidence? How can your brand create similar positive associations for your fans?

THE BALL IS IN YOUR COURT—PRACTICE DRILL #2

Stop and take note the next time you feel a jolt of "I can do that!" from a marketing message. Identify a brand that boosts your self-esteem. Examine what aspects of the brand instill confidence in you and how its marketing communicates that empowering, aspirational message to potential customers.

Takeaway for Marketers: Does your product or service inspire confidence and empowerment in your audience? Focus your messaging on how your brand helps customers achieve their personal goals, whether it's through small wins or aspirational milestones. Show them how your brand becomes part of their success story.

DNA TRAIT #3—ESCAPISM

My husband watches sports on the weekend to unwind from the stress of work during the week. Much like old-fashioned soap operas, the world of sports is brimming with drama, controversy, and surprise endings. Fans feed on this emotion and conflict, temporarily leaving their worries behind. It is the ultimate escape!

Sports fans use sports as an *escape* from the daily grind.

But it's not just about the drama—it's about the triumphs. For the duration of the game, fans become part of a cause greater than themselves, cheering for victory and celebrating success. For some, escapism has become so integral that it warrants creating a dedicated "man cave" or "she shed," a sanctuary for watching games uninterrupted.

If sports aren't your go-to escape, perhaps you can relate to one of these forms of escapism:

- **Gaming**—video games, virtual reality (VR), and online multiplayer games provide immersive experiences that transport players into other worlds.

- **Travel and Adventure**—taking vacations, road trips, or even a simple day out in nature helps people disconnect from routine and recharge.

- **Creative Arts**—hobbies like painting, writing, crafting, or photography allow people to express themselves and escape into their creativity.

- **Fitness and Physical Activities**—yoga, running, hiking, or attending group fitness classes help people de-stress while focusing on physical and mental well-being.

- **Cooking or Baking**—many people find joy and relaxation in trying new recipes or creating comfort food for themselves and their loved ones.

- **Music**—listening to music, attending concerts, or playing an instrument can transport people emotionally and mentally to another space.

- **Gardening**—for those who enjoy being outdoors, gardening offers a peaceful escape while connecting with nature.

- **Mindfulness and Meditation**—practicing mindfulness, meditation, or even guided breathing exercises offers mental clarity and escape from stress.

- **Shopping or Window Shopping**—retail therapy, whether online or in stores, provides a temporary escape and emotional boost.

- **Socializing**—spending time with friends at gatherings, cafes, or game nights is a fun way to disconnect from stress.

- **Learning Something New**—taking up new skills or hobbies, such as learning a language, trying out pottery, or joining a dance class, can be a fulfilling escape.

- **Pet Interaction**—playing with or caring for pets offers unconditional companionship and an emotional break from daily pressures.

These activities provide marketers with unique opportunities to connect with audiences by tapping into the emotions and desires associated with escapism. How a person escapes is so crucial that relationships often fail because individuals do not share at least one form of escapism or do not appreciate and support each other's escapism activities.

Immersive Escapism—The Hunger Games Campaign

One of the best examples of immersive escapism in marketing comes from Lionsgate Entertainment's campaign for *The Hunger Games* movie. Instead of relying solely on static promotional materials, the marketing team developed an interactive digital world that allowed fans to enter the universe of Panem. Through the Capitol Network website, fans could register for a District Identification Pass, which assigned them a district and occupation, fully immersing them in the fictional world created by Suzanne Collins.

Fans who registered gained access to exclusive content, updates, and social media pages for each of the 12 districts. Each district had its own Facebook page, where fans could engage with like-minded followers and stay informed about events related to the franchise. The pages were enriched with details from the story, from Capitol fashion updates to chances to run for Mayor of a District. This clever use of world-building gave fans an ongoing escape into the world of *The Hunger Games*, extending their experience beyond the movie or book.

What made the campaign especially compelling was the mystery surrounding it. The marketing withheld vital details about the movie, avoiding spoilers entirely. Fans had to see the film to fully understand what everyone was talking about—a brilliant strategy to pique curiosity while deepening the escapist experience.

Just as *The Hunger Games* campaign provided fans an immersive escape, your brand can create similar engagement opportunities. In specific applications, holding back information to intrigue fans makes them eager to participate or learn more. Do not use this case study to avoid packing your content with vital product descriptions, details, and specifications. That will cause you to lose fans fast! But when it comes to a marketing campaign, creating mystery and intrigue will leave your audience wanting more.

The Use of Humor to Escape

Great marketing doesn't always take itself too seriously and uses humor to give fans a break from the monotony of everyday life. For example:

- Old Spice's® humorous commercials have consistently captivated audiences with their offbeat humor, such as "The Man Your Man Could Smell Like." These campaigns leave fans laughing and entertained, providing lighthearted relief.

- Doritos® Super Bowl ads have become famous for their quirky humor, giving fans something to enjoy during one of the year's most highly anticipated escapist events.

Modern tools like **augmented reality (AR)** and **AI-powered engagement** take escapism even further. For instance:

- **AR Filters and Experiences**—Brands like Disney® have used AR on social media to let fans transform into characters or explore fictional worlds through their devices.

- **AI Chatbots for Interactive Storytelling**—AI-powered Chatbots can create dynamic, immersive experiences where fans feel part of the story. Imagine a chatbot that lets fans interact with their favorite characters or simulate scenarios tied to a brand's universe.

These tools create memorable moments that help fans temporarily escape the ordinary.

THE BALL IS IN YOUR COURT—PRACTICE DRILL #3

Identify your preferred escape activities. Is it reading a great book, binge-watching a series, or exercising? How do you feel during these escapes? Write down those feelings and notice when a product or service resonates with them. Effective marketing connects with these emotions to create a sense of relief or joy for its audience.

Takeaway for Marketers: Does your MX provide an escape for your audience? Consider how your marketing, sales process, product, or service delivers relief, inspiration, or entertainment to help customers escape their daily grind. Use your marketing to emphasize the emotional experience associated with your brand—creating joy, excitement, or a moment of tranquility—and position yourself as the escape they need.

DNA TRAIT #4—STATE CHANGE

Sports fans experience profound physiological and emotional shifts during games. For instance, research indicates testosterone levels surge after a victory and plummet after a defeat. These physiological responses aren't just anecdotal—they're real, measurable reactions that underscore the emotional investment in sports.

The term *eustress*—a blend of euphoria and stress—describes the positive excitement sports can elicit.[25] It's not just the die-hard fans who feel this; even casual viewers can experience moments of euphoria or disappointment, showcasing sports' universal ability to evoke strong emotions.

FANtastic Marketing evokes a *state change* in fans.

Motivational expert, author, and speaker Tony Robbins popularized the concept of physiological state change as a pivotal shift in psychological and emotional states. **According to Robbins, state change is essential for breaking old patterns and fostering personal transformation.** I attended his four-day *Unleash the Power Within* event. I can attest to his seminars, which are renowned for their dynamic energy, peer-to-peer coaching, and interactive elements, that create an environment conducive to transformational shifts, attracting attendees worldwide. And yes, in case you are wondering, I did the fire walk across hot coals! Bam!

You don't have to attend a seminar to crave a state change—it's a universal human desire. Some of us seek the catharsis of a tear-jerking movie, the adrenaline of a mountain climb, or the communal thrill of a sports game. Whether it's music, cinema, nature, or religion, these experiences help us escape our mental state and embrace something new.

In marketing, leveraging the concept of state change is a powerful tool. Take Disney World®, for example, which evokes nostalgia and wonder through its marketing campaigns like "Picture Perfect Moments," "Where Dreams Come True," and "The Happiest Place on Earth." The emphasis is on creating emotional experiences that resonate deeply with audiences. Conversely, brands like Slack® and Mailchimp often use humor and whimsy to connect with their users. For instance, Mailchimp greets users with cheerful affirmations such as "Rock on! Your email is on its way!" This playful tone fosters a lighter, more relatable connection.

Applying State Change to Your Brand With AI

State change—shifting a fan's emotions, mindset, or physical energy—is a powerful tool for building deeper connections with your audience. Here are some innovative ways brands are using AI to create these transformative moments and keep fans engaged:

1. **AI-Driven Immersive Experiences**—AI-powered AR tools like Snapchat® and Instagram transform fans' realities. For example, sports teams and brands use AR to simulate a stadium experience or allow fans to "try on" team merchandise virtually, elevating their excitement and engagement.

2. **AI for Mindfulness and Relaxation**—Meditation apps like Calm® and Headspace® use AI to suggest personalized mindfulness exercises or guided meditations based on a user's stress level.

These tools facilitate a state change by helping users relax, refocus, and feel more centered.

3. **AI-Powered Fitness Experiences**—Platforms like Peloton® and smart fitness devices use AI to dynamically adjust workout plans based on performance and goals, encouraging users to transition from feeling unmotivated to feeling energized and accomplished.

4. **Hyper-Personalized Marketing**—AI platforms such as Google Ads and Facebook utilize real-time data to display personalized ads based on a user's mood, location, or activity. For example, fans browsing Instagram during halftime may encounter an advertisement for their favorite team's merchandise, generating excitement.

5. **Virtual Concerts and Events**—Platforms like Fortnite and Roblox® have hosted AI-enhanced virtual concerts, where crowd simulations and lighting effects deepen fans' emotional connection. These immersive experiences transform fans from passive viewers to active participants.

6. **Predictive AI for Anticipation**—Sports analytics platforms and apps like ESPN® utilize AI to forecast game outcomes, sparking fan excitement and conversation. Real-time updates on a team's chances of winning keep fans emotionally engaged.

Now It's Your Turn

To effectively utilize state change, **identify the emotions** that align with your brand's ethos and your audience's desires. Are you seeking to inspire nostalgia, humor, or a sense of achievement? Brands that masterfully evoke these emotions can transform their marketing from mere messaging to impactful experiences that resonate deeply.

Learn how to relate to your fans by answering these questions on state change:

- What activities reliably create a state change for you on tough days?
- How do shared experiences like sports or concerts amplify emotional shifts for fans?
- Can your brand evoke a similar emotional journey for your audience?

THE BALL IS IN YOUR COURT—PRACTICE DRILL #4

Consider making a state change the next time you feel stuck in a rut or creatively blocked. Take a quick timeout to watch a funny cat video on YouTube, or go for a brisk walk outside. Try doing jumping jacks or turn up the music in your car. How do you feel afterward? What happens when you attempt to return to work?

Takeaway For Marketers: State change is a powerful tool for personal productivity and brand marketing. Whether it is evoking nostalgia, joy, or excitement, designing campaigns that connect emotionally helps your brand stand out. When your marketing inspires a state change, your audience will remember and associate your message with a positive, impactful experience. Engage emotions, and you will succeed loyalty.

DNA TRAIT #5—SENSE OF BELONGING

The need for a sense of belonging is one of the strongest motivators for fans, and it explains why they endure extreme conditions—sweltering heat, torrential rain, or freezing cold—to cheer for their favorite teams. The hottest I've ever been in my life was attending a late August University of Florida Gator football game at The Swamp, their iconic stadium. It was scorching, but I wouldn't have missed it for the world. The energy of 80,000+ like-minded fans, all screaming together, created a collective spirit that transcended the discomfort. At least we were all melting together!

The *sense of belonging* to a larger group fills a primal need for connection.

Most teams cultivate a sense of belonging through specific branding and rituals, strengthening the bond among fans. For instance:

- Gator fans refer to themselves as The Gator Nation, enthusiastically greeting each other with a loud "Go Gators!"
- Duke University basketball fans are renowned as The Cameron Crazies, dancing through each game with choreographed chants and cheers.
- Las Vegas Raiders fans boast The Black Hole, an adult-only, XXX-rated section of the stadium where they don elaborate, intimidating costumes.

This shared identity creates a deep connection. Fans feel part of something larger than themselves—a critical anchor in a fragmented, digital-first world.

The Role of Belonging in Modern Fan Culture

The concept of belonging has expanded significantly in the digital era. Today's fans aren't limited to physical spaces like stadiums; they connect globally through online communities.

For instance:

- The Formula 1 fan base, energized by Netflix's *Drive to Survive*, has flourished on social media. Fans exchange memes, stats, and race-day predictions, creating a virtual sense of camaraderie.
- Taylor Swift's Swifties® organize meetups, decode her lyrics, exchange friendship bracelets, and share stories online, forming a powerful global tribe transcending geography.
- Gaming communities, such as fans of Fortnite or Call of Duty®, use online matches and social networks to form bonds akin to sports fans.

This evolution demonstrates that belonging is no longer constrained by location—technology makes it accessible anywhere, anytime.

Why Fans Crave Belonging

In a fast-paced, screen-dominated world, where connections can feel shallow, fandom provides a haven of authenticity and shared purpose. As one Knicks fan shared in a *Bleacher Report* article:

> "After my divorce, I felt adrift and out of place. But being a Knicks fan gave me purpose and a place where I belonged."

This sentiment captures the essence of fandom. Whether in sports, music, or even brands, fans find kindred spirits who share their values and passions. This sense of unity feels reassuring and grounding.

Tapping Into the Power of Belonging

To leverage the sense of belonging in your marketing:

1. **Define Your Tribe**—Create a name, identity, or shared language for your community. Think *Trekkies*, *Sneakerheads*, or *HOGs*.

2. **Build Rituals**—Create traditions or rituals that unite your community. Whether through exclusive events, shared hashtags, or secret handshakes, these practices strengthen connections.

3. **Foster Inclusion**—Ensure your brand voice is inviting and connects with a diverse audience, enhancing the sentiment that everyone belongs.

4. **Engage Virtually**—Create online spaces for your fans to interact, such as Facebook groups, subreddit communities, or branded apps.

5. **Give Away or Sell Merch** – Offer branded merchandise that fans can wear, use, or proudly display. From T-shirts and hats to

mugs and stickers, merchandise transforms fans into walking ambassadors, reinforcing their connection to your brand and signaling their belonging to the tribe.

When fans feel part of a community, their loyalty skyrockets. They don't just support your brand; they champion it, recruiting others to join.

The more you become aware of your fan behaviors, the better you will understand what your fans want.

Start paying attention to your fan-related feelings, attitudes, beliefs, and needs. Ask yourself:

- What's the collective identity of your favorite brand, team, or community?
- Why do you feel connected to it?
- How can your brand foster a similar sense of community among your audience?

Five Important Truths About Fans

Ultimately, **your fans want to know you**—not the corporate identity but the people and processes that shape your company. Fans want to peek behind the curtain and understand what happens behind the scenes. When clients feel they know the real you, they can relate to and connect with you. When a customer identifies with you, they are yours for life!

Your fans want to feel good about themselves. Everyday life can be overwhelming and exhausting. Your customers seek relationships like a Celsius® beverage—refreshing, stimulating, positive, and free of artificial sweeteners. These relational interactions nourish the soul, recharge our energy, and motivate us to keep going.

Your fans seek to break free from the monotony of everyday life. They look for relationships that inject fun, humor, and lightheartedness into their experiences. No one wants to engage with brands that contribute to their frustration and workload. Instead, clients are eager to escape through your products and services, transporting them to a more relaxed and enjoyable environment.

Your fans desire to connect with you. They pay attention only to communication that conveys an emotional message, especially those that lift spirits or evoke insight and nostalgia. Engagement centers on this emotional connection.

Your fans want to belong. They seek to feel part of something larger. Most people crave a sense of belonging, which affirms our existence. Belonging reassures us that we are okay because others value what we value. I will repeat the following because the point is vital: *Although our society is **more connected than ever** through technology, our fundamental human **desire to belong to a group is stronger than ever**.* Technology, social media, and countless forms of digital engagement **do not** necessarily equate to connection.

At the heart of the FANtastic Marketing strategy is the realization that *it's not about you*. Even though you may be dying to tell your brand story and rattle off all the features of your products and services in a massive PowerPoint slide deck or two-hour online demo, your fans don't care. FANtastic Marketing is about the fans, not the brand.

It's time to stop talking, start listening, and get to know your fans.

THE BALL IS IN YOUR COURT—PRACTICE DRILL #5

Make a list of the groups you belong to (both virtual and physical).

- What do you like about being a part of the group?
- What are the benefits to you mentally, emotionally, and physically?
- How would you feel if you could no longer be part of the group?

Takeaway For Marketers: Consider your brand. How can you create a sense of belonging for your audience? What unique identity or space can you establish that makes them truly feel they belong?

Part III

PLAY BALL!

"You play ball against yourself.
Your opponent is your potential."

Bobby Knight, Indiana Hoosiers Head Coach, 1971-2000
902 Victories in NCAA Men's Basketball Games and
Three NCAA Championships

Secret #1

BE THE MVP

The Blueprint of a Modern Marketer

IN PART I: THE PRE-SEASON, we established the foundation by exploring the *Power of We*, how brands can foster deep emotional connections with their audience, and how they can transform marketing into a collaborative and fan-centric experience. Using examples like Flo from Progressive and Stitch Fix, we analyzed the critical importance of aligning marketing strategies with fans' needs, values, and emotions. We uncovered how successful brands embrace personalization, connection, and empathy to resonate with their audience.

In Part II: The Players, we focused on your fans. Exploring a fan's DNA revealed the psychological and emotional drivers that turn ordinary customers into devoted superfans. We examined identity, self-esteem, escapism, state change, and belonging as the foundations of fandom, helping you grasp what motivates and inspires your audience on a deeper level.

Now, in Part III: Play Ball!, it's time to get tactical. In this section, we directly apply the principles of superfandom to your marketing strategy. Each secret is a proven play crafted to elevate your game and deliver the results your fans expect and deserve.

We start with **Secret #1: Be the MVP—The Blueprint of a Modern Marketer.** This foundational secret sets the tone for everything to come. As we navigate today's marketing challenges fueled by technology, innovation, and relentless competition, it's vital to *think, feel, and behave like a modern marketer*. Success requires mastering your mindset, refining your actions, and building resilience to keep pace with the ever-changing landscape. Let's dive in.

KEEPING UP WITH THE JONESES

Marketing today resembles keeping up with the Joneses—not only matching your competitors' strategies but also staying ahead of constantly evolving trends and tools. When considering what it means to be a modern marketer, it's easy to feel overwhelmed, particularly if juggling multiple roles as a department of one. You're not only the creative director generating campaign ideas; you're also the copywriter crafting compelling messages, the coordinator making sure everything runs smoothly, and the analyst assessing results.

Being a modern marketer is an expansive topic that covers countless aspects of marketing in a fast-changing world. Where do you even begin?

Naturally, your initial thoughts might drift to which marketing channels to utilize, how much to invest, and what strategies to implement. Channels and tactics are the tools of the trade—they represent the "HOW" of amplifying our message. Selecting the proper channels is undoubtedly a critical component of modern marketing, but it's merely one piece of a much larger puzzle. In Secret #5, we will cover how to craft a channel and tactics strategy in depth.

Then, there's the technology: what tools and systems will you need? The hardware, software, and web applications you use daily form the foundation of your marketing operations. I've included numerous examples of technology tools throughout the book, and in Part V, there is a list of my favorite tech tools.

Beyond the stress of remaining relevant, your business must generate measurable sales results that increase market share and surpass the competition. Hold tight for Secret #9, where I will discuss how to use Google® Analytics 4 (GA4) to measure your results.

It can seem overwhelming to grasp the full extent of what is needed to be a Modern Marketer. *Remember:*

> *"You are never really playing an opponent. You are playing yourself, your own highest standards, and when you reach your limits, that is real joy."*
>
> **Arthur Ashe,** First African American man to win the singles title at Wimbledon, the US Open and the Australian Open.

There is no one-size-fits-all answer to these questions. That's why Secret #1 is so important. Rather than giving you a fish that will feed you for today, I will teach you how to fish so you can win big with FANtastic Marketing. *Hook, line, and sinker.*

MAXIMIZING YOUR HUMAN INTELLIGENCE (HI)

I ask for patience as we work through Secret #1. It may feel like we've strayed from what you expected in a book about AI-powered marketing, but I promise we are precisely on track.

This section is the most critical section of the book for your long-term success as an extraordinary and impactful marketing leader, effectively using AI tools, growing your brand, enhancing lead generation, and ultimately growing your business.

If your fans are at the *heart* of your marketing strategy, you, the marketer, are its *engine*.

To thrive in this constantly evolving landscape, you must cultivate the right mindset, develop strong execution skills, and build resilience. This serves as the blueprint for the modern marketer. It starts with maximizing your inner human intelligence (HI) and learning to *think, act, and feel* in harmony with your fans' needs and expectations.

Let's turn to the Cognitive Behavioral Therapy (CBT) model for guidance on maximizing HI. CBT is one of the most widely recognized and utilized approaches in counseling and mental health. Developed by psychologist Dr. Aaron T. Beck in the 1960s,[26] CBT is grounded in the principle that our *thoughts, feelings, and behaviors* are deeply interconnected. Over the decades, this approach has proven effective in helping individuals address various mental health challenges by understanding and reconfiguring these connections.

The Cognitive Behavioral Triangle illustrates how our thoughts, feelings, and behaviors influence one another. This model helps explain why we respond to situations in specific ways and provides a roadmap for making meaningful changes.

How does the CBT Triangle work? Each point on the triangle affects the other two. Changing one's thoughts, feelings, or behaviors creates a ripple effect that influences others. Imagine a mobile hanging above a baby crib. When you touch the elephant on the mobile, the lion and the tiger also sway. That's the CBT Triangle. Each point on the triangle causes a shift in the other two points.

THE THREE POINTS OF THE COGNITIVE BEHAVIORAL TRIANGLE

Let's dive into each part of the triangle and see how they function together. By breaking it down point by point, we'll gain a clearer picture of how thoughts, feelings, and behaviors influence one another. It's like uncovering the secret recipe behind how our minds process and respond to situations. So, grab a seat, and let's explore this fascinating connection!

1. **Thoughts—What we think about a situation shapes our interpretation of it.** For example, if you think, "I'm not good at public speaking," this thought can lead to unproductive behaviors or negative emotions. Thoughts can stem from personal beliefs, past experiences, or external circumstances. Recognizing and reframing negative or inaccurate thoughts is a key step in CBT.

2. **Feelings—Our thoughts directly influence our emotions, which in turn influence our behaviors.** For example, feeling

anxious about giving a presentation can lead to procrastinating or altogether avoiding preparation. Recognizing that our feelings are often temporary and based on our thoughts or situations enables us to manage them more effectively.

3. **Behaviors—Our actions reinforce or challenge our thoughts and feelings.** Positive actions frequently result in changes in perspective and emotional state. For instance, preparing for a presentation (even if you initially feel anxious) will foster greater confidence and a sense of accomplishment.

How can you change your thoughts, feelings, and behaviors? The following three steps provide a good starting point.

Step #1—Tackle How You Think

Modern marketers silence the noise around and within them and are **insatiably curious** about tools, tactics, strategy, and the fans themselves. This curiosity fuels the ability to connect authentically with your audience, a hallmark of the *Power of We*. It compels you to ask more profound questions, challenge assumptions, and discover new value delivery methods. **The strength and frequency of the questions you ask equal the success you achieve.**

The K.O.B.E. Framework for Curiosity

The late, great Kobe Bryant, who passed away too soon, was one of the greatest players in basketball history. He was a five-time NBA Champion and a two-time NBA Finals MVP. What you might not know about him is his penchant for curiosity.

> "Curiosity is the most important quality you can have. With curiosity, you figure things out. You are always looking for ways

to get better or reasons why certain things work...that curiosity leads you to knowledge." Kobe Bryant

In honor of Kobe, I've created **The K.O.B.E. Framework**, a series of **four questions** that ensures you approach curiosity methodically.

1. Knowledge: What do I know? More importantly, what don't I know?

2. Optimization: What existing strategies or tools could be optimized?

3. Better Execution: What processes could help us connect more deeply?

4. Efficiency: How can I deliver faster, better results?

For example, if your analytics indicate strong engagement but low lead conversions or shopping cart purchases, your curiosity drives you to investigate why. Are your calls to action compelling? Is there a disconnect between audience expectations and landing page content? Every challenge presents an opportunity to learn.

Tools to Cultivate Curiosity

In a world brimming with information, having the right tools can significantly impact your ability to keep your curiosity alive and thriving. These resources help you explore new ideas, uncover fresh insights, and remain engaged with the world around you. Let's take a closer look at some exceptional tools for nurturing curiosity.

- ✓ **Headway**—A personal growth app that offers bite-sized insights from bestselling books, enabling you to learn something new daily and remain curious about a variety of topics.

- ✔ **Perplexity AI®**—An AI-powered research assistant that answers inquiries and provides in-depth insights on nearly any subject, sparking curiosity and exploration.

- ✔ **Blinkist**—Like Headway, this app features summaries of nonfiction books, which are ideal for quickly discovering new ideas and concepts.

- ✔ **ChatGPT (OpenAI)**—Utilize ChatGPT to brainstorm ideas, explore *what-if* scenarios, or dive into unfamiliar subjects. It's like having a curiosity partner right at your fingertips.

- ✔ **Coursera®, Udemy®, and YouTube**—Platforms offering courses on various subjects, allowing you to explore your interests and develop new skills.

Step #2—Aim How You Act

In sports, a skilled archer doesn't just pull back the bowstring and hope for the best—they carefully aim, maintain their focus, and release with precision.

If you aren't familiar with archery, we can also use the analogy of an editor-in-chief at a publication. Like an editor-in-chief, a marketing leader establishes the overall vision for your brand. You determine the tone, style, and brand identity that your marketing will convey. This is where you shape how your marketing should feel, how it should communicate, and what impression it should leave.

Once the vision is established, the editor-in-chief's subsequent role is to determine a content and reporting strategy. This includes deciding how to implement the vision by effectively allocating resources. For marketing leaders, for instance, you may choose what portion of your budget will be assigned to digital channels compared to legacy media or how much emphasis to place on specific campaigns. The strategy ensures that your vision is actionable, with clear priorities and measurable objectives.

The editor-in-chief role includes a third responsibility: **reviewing and editing**. Like an article riddled with grammar and spelling errors, marketing execution is where many marketing efforts succeed or fall short. In this aspect, the editor-in-chief mentality becomes critical.

As a sales and marketing leader, your job isn't only to set the vision and strategy, but also to delve into the details and ensure impeccable execution.

I am NOT suggesting that you become a micromanager. Still, I believe in spot-checking work, providing constructive feedback, and holding your internal team and marketing partners accountable for quality.

Whether outsourcing marketing to an agency or collaborating with an in-house team, are you having meaningful review conversations? Are you taking the time to evaluate digital ads, campaigns, or collateral to ensure they align with your vision and strategy?

The old saying, "The devil is in the *details*," applies here, but let me put my spin on it: "The SALES are in the *details*." A well-executed ad or campaign can make the difference between capturing a lead and losing a potential customer. Attention to detail ensures that every aspect of your marketing aligns with your brand and drives results.

Step #3—Fuel How You Feel

Like athletes channel their emotions to stay focused under pressure, our ability to manage feelings determines how we respond to challenges. Emotions can either propel us forward like fuel in a race car or weigh us down like burdens on our shoulders.

One of my all-time favorite quotes comes from Viktor Frankl, author of the transformative book *Man's Search for Meaning*. If you haven't read it, I highly recommend it—it's one of the most significant works I've ever encountered. In it, Frankl states, "Between stimulus and response, there is a space. In that space lies our power to choose our response. In our response lies our growth and our freedom." Isn't that the truth?

Resilience begins with the ability to pause, reflect, and respond with strength and focus rather than react impulsively.

Modern marketers are resilient. They do not take every setback as a personal failure. They cultivate a thick skin to manage criticism, rejected ideas, tight budgets, and underperforming campaigns. Resilient marketers continue to move forward when the industry changes, economic downturns occur, and deadlines accumulate. They recognize the importance of balance, especially when integrating AI with HI.

Some people seem naturally resilient—stress rolls off their shoulders, and they bounce back effortlessly. Others, however, find it difficult. You might take setbacks personally, allowing challenges fester or escalate into internal drama. If this sounds familiar, here's the good news: *resilience isn't just an inherent trait; it's a skill you can cultivate.*

PRACTICING RESILIENCE

Resilience is a practice; like any skill, it develops with effort. You may have already learned resilience through significant life challenges, but it doesn't have to stem from hardship. You can actively cultivate resilience by focusing on three key areas of the CBT triangle: thinking, feeling, and behaving. Whether you begin by adjusting your thoughts, reframing your emotions, or taking small actions to shift your perspective, you can train yourself to become more adaptable and resilient.

On the path to resilience, certain traits and behaviors stand out:

✔ **Willingness to Adapt**—Stay flexible and curious in the face of change.

✔ **Problem-Solving Ability**—Approach challenges methodically, breaking them down into manageable steps.

✔ **Emotional Awareness**—Recognize and manage your emotions rather than letting them control you.

✔ **Optimism and Self-Belief**—Cultivate a positive outlook and trust in your ability to navigate difficulties.

✔ **Social Support**—Lean on your team, peers, or mentors for guidance and perspective.

- ✔ **Sense of Humor**—Perhaps one of the most underrated tools in a marketer's arsenal. Humor lightens the load, builds connections, and reminds us not to take everything so seriously.

Resilience in Action

Resilience isn't just about managing emotions; it directly impacts your work. Traits like adaptability and problem-solving lead to better decisions, such as choosing the proper marketing channels, setting appropriate campaign parameters, or targeting the right geographical audiences. Resilience ensures you stay curious and committed to improvement rather than falling into self-doubt or blame when setbacks occur.

Resilient marketers aren't just survivors but innovators, problem-solvers, and leaders. And perhaps most importantly, they know how to laugh along the way. Because in the fast-paced, high-stakes world of modern marketing, a good sense of humor might be your best secret weapon.

Tools to Build Resilience

- ✔ **Calm or Headspace**—Apps for mindfulness and meditation that teach techniques to manage stress, build mental toughness, and improve overall emotional balance.

- ✔ **BetterUp®**—A coaching platform that pairs individuals with resilience and mental performance coaches, offering structured growth plans.

- ✔ **Replika AI**—An AI-powered chatbot designed to be a supportive conversational partner, helping you reflect and process challenges in a safe, judgment-free space.

- ✔ **Gratitude Journal (Various Apps)**—Apps like **Grateful** or **Presently**® guide you through daily gratitude practices, reinforcing positive thinking and emotional resilience.

- ✔ **SuperBetter**®—A game-based resilience-building app that uses science-backed techniques to help you overcome challenges and strengthen mental fortitude.

Tools for Lifelong Learning and Exploration

- ✔ **Duolingo**®—Learning a new language stimulates curiosity and challenges your brain in innovative ways.

- ✔ **Notion AI**®—A productivity and organization tool with integrated AI features designed to help you effectively brainstorm, write, and organize your thoughts.

- ✔ **Skillshare**®—Offers classes on a variety of creative and professional topics, empowering you to explore new areas of interest and refine your skills.

- ✔ **LinkedIn**® **Learning**—Provides short courses focused on professional development, leadership, and creativity to nurture curiosity and enhance resilience in the workplace.

- ✔ **AI Dungeon**®—A creative storytelling game fueled by AI, ideal for expanding your imagination and enjoying curiosity-driven fun.

THE HOME STRETCH

Now that you've laid the foundation for modern marketing by mastering thinking, acting, and feeling, it's time to explore the next frontier: leveraging cutting-edge tools to supercharge your efforts.

In Secret #2, we'll explore the transformative potential of AI-powered marketing. By combining the mindset of a modern marketer with AI's capabilities, you'll be equipped to create innovative campaigns that are deeply aligned with your fans' needs.

THE BALL IS IN YOUR COURT—PRACTICE DRILL #6

To put the principles of Think, Act, and Feel into practice, dedicate time this week to the following drill:

1. **Think**—Conduct a brainstorming session with your team focused on curiosity. Choose one campaign and ask:
   a. What's working, and why?
   b. What's not working, and how can we test new ideas?
   c. Are there assumptions we haven't challenged?
   d. Write down every insight or question, no matter how minor.

2. **Act**—Select one area of improvement identified during the brainstorming session and take action. For example:
   a. Update the visuals or messaging of an ad campaign to better align with your fans' identity.
   b. Test a new audience segmentation strategy for email marketing.

3. **Feel**—Identify one recent setback or underperforming campaign and reframe it as a learning opportunity. What went wrong, and what did you learn? Document this as a "lesson log" to guide future decisions.

Takeaway for Marketers: Mastering the principles of *Think, Act, and Feel* goes beyond becoming a better marketer—it involves cultivating a mindset and strategy that distinguishes you in a competitive landscape. Fans connect deeply with brands that are authentic, thoughtful, and responsive. By embracing curiosity, executing with precision, and fostering resilience, you'll create campaigns that resonate significantly and yield measurable results.

Secret #2

GET IN THE GAME

Embrace and Commit to AI

DO YOU RECALL the Scarecrow from *The Wizard of Oz* singing, "If I Only Had a Brain?" It is a fitting metaphor for marketers and business leaders who sometimes feel overwhelmed and stuck in a rut, lacking the creativity, resources, or time necessary to get the job done. Whether you're a solo marketer or part of a small marketing team, it's easy to feel like you're spinning your wheels, unable to progress in a crowded, competitive landscape that moves at the speed of light.

Enter AI: your second brain with boundless creativity, knowledge, and problem-solving capabilities. Think of AI as the ultimate teammate—ready to analyze trends, brainstorm concepts, and refine your work in real time. With AI by your side, you're not just keeping pace; you're leading the charge. Whether you're a beginner or an experienced AI user, this chapter will assist you in integrating and mastering AI to elevate your business to a championship level.

AI IS A *RISING* STAR PLAYER

AI is evolving faster than nearly any other technology, with a projected compound annual growth rate (CAGR) of 36.6% from 2023 to 2030.[27] For reference, the average CAGR for tech is 10 – 15%. AI's rapid pace means businesses must commit to continuous learning and adaptation to use it responsibly and stay competitive. The following points highlight key areas to focus on when navigating the ever-changing landscape of AI.

1. **Evolving Capabilities**—AI tools are regularly updated with new features and improved performance. Staying informed ensures that you're utilizing the best tools for your needs.

2. **Regulatory Shifts**—Governments and industry organizations continuously revise AI-related regulations. Knowing the latest guidelines protects your business from compliance risks.

3. **Tailored Solutions**—AI is not one-size-fits-all. Understanding it enables you to customize tools to achieve your unique goals.

4. **Staying Ahead of Competitors**—Your rivals are also likely adopting AI. Ongoing learning keeps you one step ahead.

5. **Rising Customer Expectations**—Consumers now expect businesses to utilize advanced tools for enhanced personalization, speed, and accuracy.

Here's how to treat AI as the MVP *it can become.*

Trust but Verify

AI can process vast amounts of data and quickly generate insightful outputs but lacks human judgment. Like a teenager or rookie player learning the ropes, it may make mistakes or misunderstand information.

AI has incredible potential and is ready to come off the bench, but like a rookie with raw talent, it still needs a coach.

Always vet and confirm AI-generated insights before acting on them, especially for critical business decisions. AI may generate plausible-sounding but factually incorrect information. It could lack context or sensitivity, necessitating human intervention for nuanced language.

Use AI as an Executive Assistant, Not a CEO

AI excels at handling tasks like data analysis, automating repetitive workflows, and generating content. However, it depends on human direction, context, and strategy. Viewing AI as an executive assistant allows you to delegate research, data aggregation, and drafting communications while keeping your team's final decision-making and quality control in mind.

Match Tasks to the Right Tools

Not all AI tools are equal, and each excels in different areas. For instance:

- Use ChatGPT or similar tools to craft content or answer queries.
- Leverage DALL·E® for generating creative visuals.
- Employ Tableau AI® or Power BI® AI for data visualization and analysis.
- Implement Hootsuite Insights for social media sentiment tracking.

The output becomes more precise and actionable by aligning the task with the most appropriate AI tool; it results in increased accuracy and actionability.

Continuous Monitoring and Feedback

AI learns and adapts most effectively when guided by feedback. To enhance its results, track its performance, pinpoint areas for improvement, and refine its tasks or input prompts.

What Can AI Do for You?

- Assign AI to compile a list of trends in your industry. Review and verify the information before sharing it with stakeholders.
- Use AI to draft emails or reports, but ensure you edit and approve the final versions to maintain the tone and accuracy consistent with your brand.

- Delegate repetitive tasks, like invoice processing or basic customer service inquiries, while keeping oversight to manage exceptions or escalations.

By treating AI as a supportive assistant rather than a decision-maker, you can harness its strengths while safeguarding against its limitations—like guiding a teenager through the complexities of the real world. This book's use cases and technology suggestions exemplify safe, responsible, and successful ways to utilize AI.

AI—YOUR BRAINSTORMING SLAM DUNK

AI is a slam dunk for brainstorming new ideas or optimizing campaigns. Think of it as the ultimate teammate—always ready to assist and never running out of energy. The following list (though not exhaustive by any means) outlines ways to leverage AI for idea generation.

1. **Break Out of a Rut**—Tools like ChatGPT or Jasper AI® can kick-start creativity by offering unique perspectives.
   - ✔ For example, input "list 10 creative ways to promote a summer sale at my nail salon" and receive suggestions like "host a tropical-themed virtual event" or "offer discounts tied to daily weather patterns."

2. **Refine Your Ideas**—Tools like Grammarly® ensure clarity in writing, while Canva's Magic Resize instantly resizes visuals for various platforms.
   - ✔ For example, if you're drafting a blog post about summer skincare tips, Grammarly can suggest improvements for tone and grammar, while Canva's Magic Resize can quickly adapt

your blog header image into an Instagram Story or Facebook Ad format.

3. **Bounce Ideas Off AI**—Experiment with different taglines, ad copy, or social media posts to determine which resonates most.
   - ✔ For example, if you're marketing a new outdoor grill, you could ask an AI tool, "Which tagline hits harder: 'Master the Flames, Rule the Cookout' or 'Every Grill, A Victory'?" The AI can analyze which option carries more impact and aligns best with your audience's preferences.

AI – RUNS THROUGH THE TAPE

AI's role extends beyond brainstorming; it also involves executing strategies with precision. Here's how to leverage AI across various marketing disciplines:

1. **Trendspotting**—Use tools like BuzzSumo® to identify trending topics and generate timely content.
   - ✔ For instance, if BuzzSumo indicates a spike in searches for "Top Hiking Gear for Summer Adventures," you can create a blog post featuring essential outdoor gear and safety tips to align with the trend.

2. **Audience Insights**—Platforms such as HubSpot® analyze data to recommend themes tailored for your customers.
   - ✔ For instance, if HubSpot reveals a growing interest in "Simple Home Gym Setups" among your audience, you could produce short videos showcasing effective home workout routines using minimal equipment.

3. **Campaign Optimization**—Tools like Surfer SEO® ensure that your blog ranks well in search engines. AI analytics platforms monitor engagement and suggest improvements.
   - ✔ For example, if your blog post "Best Backyard BBQ Recipes" attracts views but not shares, Surfer SEO might recommend incorporating eye-catching images or enhancing the introduction to boost reader retention.

4. **Enhance Personalization**—AI can analyze customer data to create targeted campaigns that resonate with individual preferences.
   - ✔ For example, a coffee shop could use AI to send latte art tutorials to customers who frequently purchase specialty drinks.

AI'S BROADER ROLE NOT JUST MARKETING

AI isn't just the star player in marketing; it's valuable across all aspects of business:

1. **Operations**—Tools such as Zapier® automate workflows, saving time on repetitive tasks.

2. **Sales**—AI CRM tools like HubSpot or Salesforce® Einstein analyze buyer behavior to prioritize leads.

3. **Customer Support**—AI-powered chatbots offer 24/7 customer service by handling FAQs and escalating complex queries to human agents.

SHOW UP TO PRACTICE

Continuous learning is essential for effectively integrating AI into your business. Staying current is vital. You can accomplish this by following industry news, joining AI-focused forums, or subscribing to newsletters from trusted sources like *OpenAI* or *MIT Technology Review*.

Businesses should commit to continuous learning in AI by regularly investing in training programs, webinars, or certifications to enhance their teams' understanding of it.

Experimentation is crucial; dedicating resources to exploring new AI tools and evaluating their applications can uncover improvement opportunities. Collaborating with experts, such as AI specialists or consultants, provides valuable guidance for implementation and updates. Finally, fostering a learning culture within your organization encourages employees to share insights, stay curious, and remain engaged with emerging technologies. By embracing this approach, your business ensures it not only effectively leverages AI today but also adapts to its transformative potential in the future.

ESSENTIAL SKILLS TO SUCCEED WITH AI

Integrating AI into your workflow isn't just about using the tools—it's about using them *well*. Success with AI relies on a blend of technical know-how, strategic thinking, and soft skills that bridge the gap between human creativity and machine efficiency.

Here are some key skills to focus on:

1. **Editing and Refinement**—AI can generate content, analyze data, or offer solutions, but it often needs a human touch to refine and polish the results. A skilled editor means spotting inaccuracies, aligning outputs with your brand's voice, and ensuring clarity and precision.
   - ✔ For example, after using ChatGPT to draft a blog post, a sharp editor can fine-tune the tone, remove repetition, and enhance flow for maximum impact.

2. **Critical Thinking**—AI excels at pattern recognition and data processing, but it doesn't replace human judgment. Evaluating AI-generated suggestions critically is essential to avoid errors or unintended consequences.
   - ✔ For example, when an AI tool suggests marketing strategies, a critical thinker can assess whether they align with long-term business goals.

3. **Prompt Engineering**—The quality of AI outputs often depends on the caliber of your inputs. Crafting clear, specific, and goal-oriented prompts can make all the difference.
   - ✔ For example, instead of asking, "Write about summer sales," a strong prompt would be, "Write a fun and engaging email subject line for a summer sale targeting young professionals."

4. **Data Literacy**—AI thrives on data, and understanding how to read, interpret, and apply data insights is essential. This skill ensures that AI-driven analytics lead to actionable results.
   - ✔ For example, a data-literate user can use an AI analytics dashboard to identify trends and pivot strategies based on key performance metrics.

5. **Adaptability and Curiosity**—We covered these skills in Secret #1, and now you understand why I delved into these topics! It wasn't just for you to become an effective marketer but also because AI tools evolve rapidly, and staying curious and adaptable is essential to keeping up. Being open to learning new tools and experimenting with AI applications will give you an edge.
   - ✔ For instance, exploring new features in tools like MidJourney® or Surfer SEO can uncover innovative ways to enhance your content strategy.

6. **Ethical Oversight**—AI raises ethical concerns about bias, privacy, and transparency. Understanding the ethical implications of AI outputs and usage is crucial for ensuring responsible implementation.
   - ✔ For example, if an AI tool generates customer messaging, an ethical lens ensures the language is inclusive, respectful, and aligned with your brand values.

7. **Creative Vision**—AI can help execute creative ideas, but the spark of creativity originates from HI. A clear vision ensures that AI outputs align with your goals and storytelling.
   - ✔ For instance, when generating visuals with Stable Diffusion or Jasper Art, a strong creative direction ensures the images align with your campaign theme and brand aesthetic.

These skills involve merging **HI with AI** for more thoughtful, impactful outcomes. Master them, and you won't just utilize AI—you'll *lead* with it.

THE LIMITS OF BUILT-IN AI—WHY AI-FIRST TOOLS SHINE

As marketers, we're fortunate to live in a time when artificial intelligence is woven into countless software platforms, from social media schedulers to email marketing tools. These embedded AI features can be beneficial, offering conveniences like auto-suggested headlines, grammar checks, and simple sentence rewrites. However, these tools are often designed as add-ons rather than as the centerpiece of the software.

This distinction matters because when AI is just one feature among many, it tends to **lack the depth and precision** of AI-first platforms like ChatGPT, Jasper AI, or Scribe.

Built-In AI—Good, But Not Great

Built-in AI tools often focus on quick wins:

- Suggesting subject lines for emails.
- Offering stock recommendations for social media captions.
- Flagging grammatical errors or proposing minor rewrites.

While these tools can accelerate repetitive tasks, their accuracy and ability to understand nuanced requests often fall short. For instance, if you ask a built-in AI tool in an email platform to rewrite a sentence, you might receive a clunky or overly simplified result that misses your intended tone or message. These tools frequently struggle to maintain context, failing to grasp the subtle points you're trying to convey.

Why AI-First Tools Stand Out

In contrast, AI-first platforms like ChatGPT excel because they are specifically designed to manage complex language tasks, foster deep ideation, and facilitate nuanced communication. Here's why:

1. **Focus on AI as a Core Function**—Tools dedicated to AI emphasize understanding and delivering high-quality output. When you ask an AI-first tool to rewrite a sentence, it doesn't merely shuffle words around—it comprehends your intent and aims to maintain your tone, nuance, and original meaning.

2. **Customizability and Context Awareness**—AI-first tools are designed with advanced natural language processing (NLP) models, which allow them to consider the broader context of a paragraph or document. This contextual awareness ensures that your rewritten text aligns with your main point instead of feeling disjointed.

3. **Greater Range of Applications**—AI-first platforms offer flexibility that built-in AI tools can't match. From creating long-form blogs and generating SEO keywords to brainstorming entire marketing campaigns, these tools act as comprehensive marketing partners rather than simple task assistants.

4. **Regular Updates and Refinements**—AI-focused platforms invest significantly in research and updates to stay at the forefront. For instance, the latest versions of tools like ChatGPT have been trained on billions of data points, enhancing their capacity to understand complex queries and provide accurate results.

5. **More Human-Like Output**—Built-in AI often provides robotic, formulaic responses, while AI-first tools strive to emulate

human language, tone, and thought processes. This results in an authentic, polished, and professional first draft. Remember, the writing quality of any AI tool is as good as the prompt you enter and is always, at best, a first draft. You must use your HI to refine and edit the copy into a final draft.

The Risk of Settling for Good Enough

Relying solely on built-in or add-on AI tools may save time in the short term, but it can lead to generic or uninspired content. Worse, inaccuracies or poorly phrased outputs can weaken your messaging and frustrate your audience.

Marketers who aim for impactful campaigns should consider built-in AI a supplement rather than a substitute for dedicated tools. AI-first platforms are a better investment for tasks that demand creativity, precision, and strategic insight.

How to Leverage Both Effectively

You don't have to choose one over the other—many marketers use built-in AI for quick tasks and reserve dedicated tools for higher-stakes projects. For example:

- **Built-In AI**—Use it to auto-suggest hashtags, correct typos, or identify trending topics.

- **AI-First**—Use tools like ChatGPT to rewrite complex passages, develop a full content calendar, or generate campaign ideas.

By understanding the strengths and limitations of each, you can create a hybrid approach that saves time while ensuring top-tier results. Think of built-in AI tools as the Swiss Army knife of marketing—they're versatile and handy but not designed for complex work. On the other hand, AI-first tools are your specialized instruments tailored for precision, creativity, and innovation.

When accuracy and nuance matter—whether it's refining a brand voice or crafting an impactful message—AI-first platforms offer the expertise and reliability you need to stand out. The result? *FANtastic Marketing that feels thoughtful, relevant, and genuinely connected to your audience.*

THE BALL IS IN YOUR COURT—PRACTICE DRILL #7

Choose a task or challenge your business often encounters—something repetitive, time-consuming, or creative. Investigate two AI tools that claim to assist with this task. For instance, you might investigate AI tools for generating blog content, creating visuals, or analyzing customer feedback. Evaluate each tool using the same task and compare their outputs. Assess the tools based on the following criteria: ease of use, accuracy, relevance to your needs, and overall value for your business. Rate each tool on a scale from 1 to 5 in each category and select the one that aligns best with your goals.

Takeaway for Marketers: Spend time exploring and evaluating AI tools firsthand. This will help you understand their potential and limitations. By directly engaging with the tools, you will gain practical insights into how they can improve your processes, save time, and elevate your marketing efforts. The more familiar you are with AI, the better prepared you'll be to utilize it as a key player on your team.

Secret #3

STEP UP TO THE PLATE

Dig Deep to Unlock the Secrets of Your SuperFans

HOW WELL DO you know your fans? Can you name their top three favorite apps, preferred social platforms, and the types of products and services they trust the most? Do you know where they live and work? What are their favorite restaurants and shopping spots, and what make and model of cars do they drive? How and where do they get their news? Are you aware of what they enjoy doing in their free time and what values guide their lifestyles?

The first step to building a remarkable brand is to step up to the plate and gather deep insights into your fans. We've all seen a television commercial and thought, "That company doesn't get it (or me)." Whether it's a poorly targeted ad or a tone-deaf message, these missteps often occur due to a lack of audience understanding. The good news? You can avoid these pitfalls by combining traditional human intelligence with modern AI tools to gain a 360-degree view of your fans.

THE POWER OF KNOWING YOUR FANS

Imagine you're having a conversation with someone who only talks about themselves. Do you want to keep listening? Customers feel the same way when brands focus solely on their products and fail to consider their audience's needs. By learning to *listen* to your fans digitally and face-to-face, you can create a genuine connection that drives loyalty and engagement.

Ask yourself:

- When did I last analyze customer feedback or insights using GA4?
- How often do I review social media metrics to identify trends in customer conversations?
- Can I describe the psychological motivations that drive my customers to choose my brand over others?

FANTASTIC MARKETING IS OBJECTIVE AND ETHICAL

Creating fan profiles and personas isn't about judging one group as better than another—it's about understanding them without bias. As marketers, we must approach this process with complete neutrality, focusing solely on the lifestyles, needs, and passions that drive each group.

This objectivity is essential for discovering why a particular group connects with your brand. Even if their preferences or beliefs don't align with yours, your role is to understand them, not judge them. To effectively use The Fan Factor strategies, you must identify the messaging and visuals that resonate with your audience.

In addition, it's crucial to be brutally honest, granular, and specific about fan preferences; otherwise, this process will fail. You and your company must be able to quickly and accurately complete the statement: "Our fans buy from us because...."

Until you can answer WHO buys your product and WHY, you don't know your fans as well as you should.

You may be worried that limiting your audience to a few demographic or psychographic niches restricts appeal and potential sales. However, I can tell you from many years of experience helping brands attract more traffic, generate leads, and boost sales that the exact opposite is true. Being specific about your market will enable you to increase sales.

Why is this? It's due to the high costs associated with marketing to a broad audience. Unless you are Nike, Coca-Cola®, or Target®, you likely don't have the budget or staff resources to market to the masses. If you attempt to sell to a broad audience with a smaller budget, your money will be wasted, as your message will get lost in the flood of information produced by the vast corporate marketing giants that continuously bombard our multitasking minds with unlimited advertising. Targeting your message to the exact group that can support you makes much more sense, both in terms of budget and results.

If you're skeptical, reread Part II and answer this: What did you have for breakfast one week ago today? When did you last go shopping and forget your shopping list (I can't be the only one!)? What about the last time you forgot a meeting or a conference call you noted was about to begin only 15 minutes ago?

Your brain's functioning should be evidence enough that memorable impressions are hard to form. That's why you cannot market to everyone and be memorable. **The way to build your brand, gain new customers, and blow past your sales goals is to identify a fan niche and go 100 miles deep in that niche.** You must know your fans so well that you speak with the same voice they do and leave them wondering, "How did you know what I needed?"

While audience profiling is powerful, it must be used responsibly. When gathering and analyzing customer data, businesses must adhere to ethical practices and comply with legal regulations to ensure transparency, respect for privacy, and proper data handling. Ethically, companies should obtain explicit customer consent, collect only necessary data, and communicate how it will be used. Data should be anonymized when possible to protect individuals, and companies must avoid using data exploitative or discriminatory ways.

Legal compliance differs by region and industry, encompassing regulations like the EU's General Data Protection Regulation (GDPR), the California Consumer Privacy Act (CCPA) in the US, and sector-specific laws like HIPAA for health data. These laws mandate that businesses provide customers access to their data, allow them to opt out of data collection, and ensure secure data storage and processing. Additional best practices involve conducting regular audits, training employees on data privacy standards, encrypting sensitive information, and appointing a Data Protection Officer (DPO) when necessary. Following these ethical and legal standards can foster customer trust while shielding themselves from reputational and legal risks.

BUILDING FAN PERSONAS

Your fan profiles should include **demographic *and* psychographic details:**

- **Demographics**—Age, gender identity, cultural heritage, household income, location, occupation, etc.

- **Psychographics**—Values, interests, lifestyles, and motivations of consumer buying behavior.

A complete fan profile should minimally contain the following demographic data (and perhaps more items specific to your business):

✔ Age range
✔ Cultural Background/Heritage
✔ Education Level
✔ Gender Identity
✔ Geographic Location
✔ Household Income Range
✔ Household Size Range
✔ Interests/Hobbies
✔ Lifestyle Choices
✔ Occupation/Industry/Job Title

USE THE VALS™ FRAMEWORK TO GUIDE HI

When building fan personas, don't stop with basic demographic information such as age range, gender identity, and cultural background/heritage. Use HI to listen for psychographic clues about your fans' values and beliefs.

The field of psychographics studies psychological motivation related to consumer buying behavior. Psychographics first appeared in the 1960s with the work of Arnold Mitchell, who developed the original VALS (Values and Lifestyles Study) model.

Mitchell's early system was updated in 1989 by three progressive research organizations: SRI International, Stanford University, and the University of California at Berkeley[28] to reflect changing consumer behaviors.

According to the VALS study, "motivations and resources determine how people express themselves in the marketplace. People buy products and services and seek experiences that fulfill their characteristic preferences and give shape, substance, and satisfaction to their lives."

VALS categorizes consumers into three groups:

1. **Ideals Customers**—*Principles and values* guide these customers. They seek products that align with their deeply held beliefs, which are based on guiding principles such as quality, sustainability, or being locally owned and operated.
   - ✓ **What to Listen For:** Questions about how a product is made, where the company is located, or the company's mission and values.

- ✔ **How to Respond:** Provide facts about your product's sustainability, production process, or reliability.

2. **Achievement Customers**—These customers are motivated by *success and social recognition.* They buy products that symbolize achievement or elevate their status.
   - ✔ **What to Listen For:** Comments about popular trends, premium options, or competitor comparisons.
   - ✔ **How to Respond:** Highlight your product's aspirational qualities or endorsements from respected figures.

3. **Self-Expression Customers**—These customers value *individuality and creativity.* They want products that reflect their unique style or personality.
   - ✔ **What to Listen For:** Statements about wanting something *different* or *fun.*
   - ✔ **How to Respond:** Emphasize customization options or unique aspects of your product.

By listening for these motivations, your team can adapt their messaging to resonate with what truly matters to your fans.

CREATE FAN PROFILES WITH AI INSIGHTS

Creating fan profiles involves more than compiling raw data. It also involves finding actionable patterns and building strategies around them. Modern tools make this process faster and more reliable. Here's how to harness the power of technology for fan profiling.

Step #1—Set the Stage for Creativity and HI Collaboration

Begin with an internal team meeting to share knowledge and generate ideas. Consult and listen to your front-line employees, such as customer service representatives and sales leaders, for insights on your customers' wants, needs, and desires. Utilize AI platforms like **Looker Studio** or **Tableau** to visualize customer data trends. Provide your team with markers, Post-it® flip charts, and interactive dashboards to brainstorm the HI insights.

Step #2—Incorporate AI-Driven Tools

Supplement traditional methods like surveys and focus groups with insights from AI tools. Platforms like Sprinklr® and Brandwatch analyze customer interactions across channels, identifying trends you might miss manually.

Step #3—Refine Through Visualization

Encourage small teams to develop detailed fan profiles by assigning each profile a name, such as Sally or Juan, and visualizing a face. Use AI dashboards to display demographic and psychographic patterns. After collecting data, consolidate the findings into a centralized document and identify trends. AI can assist by grouping data into actionable segments, making it easier to identify opportunities.

HYPOTHETICAL CASE STUDY

This fictional example illustrates how small businesses can combine AI-driven tools with human intelligence to understand better and engage with their customer base.

Business Overview

BeanBrew Café, a fictional small coffee shop in Austin, Texas, faces stiff competition from larger chains. To stand out, it leverages AI-powered tools and human insights to gather actionable data, deepen customer connections, and create personalized experiences.

Challenge

The café has a limited marketing budget and steep overhead costs. Staffing is lean, and the shop must turn a profit quickly. Competition is fierce and dominated by big, national brands.

Solution: Combining AI and HI

BeanBrew utilizes AI-powered tools like Sprout Social® to track online discussions about the café and its competitors. These tools examine hashtags, comments, and mentions to identify trends and sentiments. AI automatically recognizes and measures positive, neutral, or negative emotions. Meanwhile, the café's team collects comments to capture nuanced feedback that AI may overlook, such as frequent references to a "cozy atmosphere" and "friendly baristas." **Insights from this process indicate that remote workers visit the café for its ambiance but want more charging stations and faster Wi-Fi.**

The café integrates GA4 on its website and app to track customer interactions. GA4 uses machine learning to highlight customer segments, such as frequent visitors or first-time users. The team cross-references AI insights with real-world observations, such as in-store ordering trends. **This reveals a high click-through rate for seasonal beverage promotions, which correlates with in-store traffic spikes.**

Open-ended response surveys sent via Typeform® are enriched with natural language processing (NLP) to analyze responses. NLP identifies recurring themes such as "sustainability" and "eco-friendly practices" in customer feedback. The team complements this by personally interviewing regular customers to validate survey findings and gather deeper qualitative insights. **These efforts reveal**

that customers value sustainability, reflected in their purchases of reusable cups and eco-friendly products.

BeanBrew runs an advertising campaign to attract new customers using Google Ads AI and Facebook Ads AI. These platforms automatically optimize ad targeting based on demographic data, geographic locations, and customer interests. Google Ads AI identifies high-performing keywords such as "cozy coffee shop Austin" and adjusts bids for improved ROI. Facebook Ads AI targets users interested in local events, sustainability, and remote work. The marketing team ensures that ad copy and designs align with BeanBrew's authentic voice. **Campaigns centered on sustainability and seasonal promotions achieve the highest engagement.**

Results

A new "Eco-Friendly Autumn" campaign emphasizes sustainability, reusable cups, and seasonal drinks, resulting in a 30% increase in marketing ROI due to AI-driven ad optimization and human-focused messaging. An enhanced customer experience with more charging stations and upgraded Wi-Fi boosts foot traffic among remote workers by 20%. Personalized emails based on GA4 insights provide discounts on frequently purchased items, improving retention by 25% within six months. New plant-based options, such as oat milk matcha lattes, are promoted on social media through Facebook Ads AI, leading to a 45% increase in social media engagement as customers share posts about the new offerings.

THE BALL IS IN YOUR COURT—PRACTICE DRILL #8

Choose a product or brand that doesn't appeal to you. You earn bonus points if this brand offers a product or service you believe wastes time or money—something you would never purchase or be interested in. Put aside your judgment of its worth or value. Examine the fan base for the product. Develop a demographic and psychographic profile of that fan. Then, assess the product's messaging and rate its marketing on a scale from 1 to 10. A score of 1 indicates no understanding of its fan base, while a score of 10 shows mastery in knowing its fans and delivering exactly what they want.

Takeaway For Marketers: Learn to set aside personal biases and approach audience analysis objectively and empathetically. Understanding your fanbase isn't about your preferences; it's about forming a deep connection with theirs. By understanding who your fans are and why they engage with your brand, you can create marketing that resonates deeply and authentically.

Secret #4

KEEP YOUR EYE ON THE BALL

Turn Your Website into a Fan Magnet

ONE OF MY FAVORITE childhood memories is my dad coaching me to hit a baseball. We lived in Orlando, FL, with a large backyard enclosed by a chain-link fence. Dad would face me toward the empty lot next door, pitching ball after ball while repeating, "Keep your eye on the ball." My mission? To hit the ball over the chain-link fence into the empty lot. The reward? Ice cream. Now, I'm not athletically gifted, but that summer, I connected the bat with the ball enough times to earn plenty of trips to Dairy Queen.

That summer instilled in me discipline; a quality essential for anyone aiming to implement FANtastic Marketing. Just as I had to focus on the ball during those batting practices, you must keep your eye on the ball in marketing, avoiding distractions from every shiny new tool or tactic. Sure, experimenting with new approaches and technologies like AI is essential, and flexibility is crucial, but allowing fragmentation to dominate your strategy is a mistake. We know marketing leaders or business owners who let trendy tech or shiny new consultants guide their decision-making. The best practice is introducing new technologies in phases and applying them to one campaign or marketing tactic until thoroughly tested.

YOUR WEBSITE—THE QUARTERBACK OF YOUR MX

I can't tell you how often I meet marketing leaders and business owners who are up to speed on the latest social media trends or tech gadgets, but when I visit their websites, I'm floored by what's missing. Their sites lack the hallmarks of success, whether usability, design, or mobile optimization.

Here's what I tell them, and now I'll tell you: *until your website is a WOW, don't spend time or money on other marketing tactics or technology*. You might as well roll down your car window on the highway and throw cash out at 80 miles per hour.

FANtastic marketers prioritize their website above everything else.

This may seem obvious and outdated advice. Still, to this day, my team and I meet business owners every week whose websites need to be updated, visually unappealing, hard to navigate, and not mobile-friendly. That's why I feel compelled to drive this point home. Before you brush off this advice, take a moment to be brutally honest with yourself. *On a scale of 1 to 10, how effective is your website?* If your answer isn't a 9 or 10, keep reading—because this is where the real work begins.

10 CHARACTERISTICS OF A GAME-WINNING, WOW WEBSITE

A winning website isn't just about good looks—it's about creating an MX that captivates visitors, communicates value instantly, and converts curiosity into action. Below are 10 essential characteristics to help your website stand out, deliver a WOW MX, and drive results.

Characteristic #1—Crystal Clear Messaging

Users form an impression of a website in as little as 0.05 seconds[29]—faster than the blink of an eye. This split-second judgment highlights the importance of clearly stating *who you are*, *what you do*, and, most importantly, *why potential fans should care*. Use concise, compelling, and conversational copy, and avoid jargon. Remember to assume a relationship with your fans! Speak directly to pain points and offer immediate solutions.

- Use bold headlines that emphasize your value proposition.
- Include subheadings to break down services and benefits.
- Write in the second person ("you," "your") to make it relatable.

AI/Tech Game Changers:

✔ **ChatGPT (OpenAI)**—Generate compelling headlines, value propositions, and website copy tailored to your audience.

- ✔ **Copy.ai®**—Create benefit-driven, conversion-focused messaging for landing pages.

- ✔ **Jasper AI**—Tone-customized messaging that aligns with your brand voice.

Pro Tip: Use a value proposition statement prominently on your homepage to communicate the unique benefits you provide. For example, summarize your unique value using a "hero statement" at the top of your homepage. Test phrases like "Helping [audience] solve [problem] with [solution]." Test your messaging by asking someone unfamiliar with your business to describe what you do after a 10-second glance.

Characteristic #2—Mobile-First Design

With over 50% of web traffic coming from mobile devices, your site needs to work flawlessly on screens of all sizes.[30] Mobile optimization isn't optional—it's foundational.

- Ensure clickable elements (buttons, links) are large enough for thumbs.

- Avoid pop-ups or features that are hard to close on mobile, or that cover too much of the screen, blocking buttons and menus. Test forms and calls-to-action to ensure they're user-friendly on small screens.

AI/Tech Game Changers:

- ✔ **Durable**—Builds mobile-friendly websites quickly and effectively.

✔ **Wix ADI®**—Uses AI to create responsive designs optimized for mobile.

✔ **Bookmark AiDA**—Ensures mobile-friendly layouts automatically.

Pro Tip: Run a mobile huddle to review your website on multiple devices and check for ease of navigation, readability, and form functionality. Use Google's Mobile-Friendly Test tool to evaluate your site.

Characteristic #3—Blazing Fast Loading Speed

40% of users will abandon a site if loading takes over three seconds.[31] Research indicates that a delay of even one second can reduce conversions by 7%.[32] Speed isn't just a convenience; it's a necessity. Slow websites frustrate visitors, signal unprofessionalism, and impact Search Engine Optimization (SEO) rankings.

- Compress images without sacrificing quality.
- Enable browser caching and use a content delivery network (CDN).
- Minimize JavaScript and CSS files.

AI/Tech Game Changers:

✔ **Google PageSpeed Insights**—Analyzes your website and provides actionable suggestions to improve load speed.

✔ **NitroPack®**—AI-powered performance optimization for improving speed and reducing load times.

Pro Tip: Aim for a load time of under 2 seconds. Use a WordPress® plugin like WPSmush to compress images and improve page load speed.

Characteristic #4—Prominent Call-To-Actions (CTAs)

A well-positioned CTA skyrockets conversion rates by 80%.[33] CTAs are the linchpins of your website's lead-generation success. They should tell visitors exactly what to do next and be impossible to miss.

- Use action verbs like "Call Now," "Get Your Free Consultation," or "Request Information."

- Position CTAs at logical points: above the fold, mid-scroll, and end of pages.

- Ensure CTAs contrast visually with the rest of the page.

AI/Tech Game Changers:

✔ **ChatGPT**—Quickly brainstorm unique call-to-action keywords, phrases, and headlines.

✔ **Jasper AI**—Craft action-oriented CTA copy designed to convert.

✔ **Optimizely**®—A/B test CTA designs and placements to maximize conversions.

Pro Tip: Position CTAs above the fold and use contrasting colors for buttons to make them stand out like a game-winning jersey.

Characteristic #5—Social Proof and Trust Elements

92% of website users check the reviews FIRST before they buy a product online.[34] Trust is your biggest asset. Visitors want proof that you deliver results. To build credibility, showcase testimonials, reviews, awards, and affiliations.

- Display testimonials and success stories prominently.
- Include badges for certifications, awards, or affiliations.
- Showcase reviews and ratings from trusted platforms like Google or Yelp.

AI/Tech Game Changers:

✔ **Looka®**—AI-generated professional logos and branding to build credibility.

✔ **TrustPulse®**—An AI-driven tool that displays real-time social proof notifications like recent purchases or sign-ups.

✔ **Tidio®**—Chatbots that can highlight customer testimonials or reviews in real time.

Pro Tip: In addition to a dedicated Testimonials or Reviews webpage, sprinkle testimonials, reviews, and awards throughout the website on your most visited and popular pages.

Characteristic #6—User-Friendly Lead Forms

Decreasing lead form input fields from 11 to 4 increases conversions by a whopping 120%.[35] Your forms serve as the gateway to conversions. They ought to be welcoming, user-friendly, quick to fill out, and simple to submit.

- Keep fields to a minimum (e.g., name, email, phone, comments/ questions).
- Use smart defaults and dropdowns for ease.
- Include reassurance with privacy statements like "We'll never share your information."

AI/Tech Game Changers:

✔ **Typeform**—AI-driven interactive forms that are engaging and easy to use.

✔ **Formstack**®—Create customizable forms with AI-driven optimization to achieve higher conversion rates.

✔ **Zapier**—Automate lead capture from forms directly into your CRM.

Pro Tip: Include multiple options for visitors to contact you, including phone, text, or chat, for added flexibility.

Characteristic #7—SEO-Optimized Content

Google is the 800-pound gorilla of website traffic, with 92% of all global traffic.[36] What's the purpose of an excellent website if it can't be found in Google searches? Incorporate SEO best practices to ensure your site appears in the Google SERPs (search engine results page) when potential customers seek your product or services.

- Research and include target keywords naturally throughout your site.
- Optimize page titles, meta descriptions, and headings.
- Create content that answers common customer questions.

AI/Tech Game Changers:

✔ **Surfer SEO**—Provides AI recommendations for keywords, headings, and structure for better rankings.

✔ **SEMrush® or Moz®**—Analyze and optimize your content for search engines.

✔ **RankMath® or Yoast®**—WordPress plugins for on-page SEO optimization with AI-powered insights.

Pro Tip: Regularly publish valuable, keyword-rich content like blogs or FAQs that address common customer queries.

Characteristic #8—Intuitive Navigation

94% of users say easy navigation is the most crucial feature of a website, and most visitors look at your main navigation for only SIX seconds.[37] A confusing site structure is like fumbling the ball—users will leave if they can't find what they need. Simplify navigation to create a seamless experience.

- Use a clear menu structure with logical categories.
- Include a search bar for users seeking specific information.

- Make your most important pages (e.g., Contact, Services) easy to access from any point.

AI/Tech Game Changers:

✔ **Hotjar®**—Use AI-driven heatmaps to identify navigation bottlenecks and improve site flow.

✔ **Optimizely**—A/B test navigation menus to enhance user experience.

✔ **Google Analytics**—Analyze visitor behavior to optimize navigation paths.

Pro Tip: Include a 2-click rule—any page should be accessible within two clicks from the homepage. Even better if its 1-click.

Characteristic #9—Compelling Visuals

A picture is worth a thousand words—or a thousand leads, given that high-quality product photos have a 94% higher conversion rate! 75% of online shoppers rely on high-quality images to make purchasing decisions.[38] Your visuals are your game highlights. Photos and videos must be high-quality, relevant, and evoke emotion.

- Use professional, on-brand photography rather than stock images.
- Incorporate video content to explain services or share customer stories.
- Ensure visuals are optimized to maintain fast load speeds.

AI /Tech Game Changers:

✔ **Canva Magic Resize**—Create visually engaging images tailored to your website dimensions.

✔ **Adobe® Sensei**—AI-powered design suggestions to ensure visually striking layouts.

✔ **Pexels AI Search®**—Quickly find high-quality visuals that align with your brand.

Pro Tip: Use visuals to guide the user's eye toward CTAs or essential information.

Characteristic #10: Analytics-Driven Insights

Businesses relying on data analytics lead to 5X faster decision-making and are 23 times more likely to acquire customers and 6 times more likely to retain them.[39] A lead-generating, WOW-worthy website evolves continuously. Regularly analyzing user behavior can reveal opportunities to improve conversions.

- Monitor bounce rates, session durations, and conversion paths.
- Conduct A/B testing on elements like CTAs, forms, or headlines.

AI/Tech Game Changers:

✔ **Hotjar**—Visualize user behavior through session recordings and heatmaps.

✔ **Google Analytics**—Provides insights into visitor traffic, bounce rates, and conversion paths.

✓ **HubSpot CRM**—AI-driven dashboards to monitor lead sources and website performance.

Pro Tip: Use Google Tag Manager's event tracking to track key events (conversions) in GA4, and use heatmaps to see where visitors click most.

THE FINAL SCORE

Your website will deliver a WOW-worthy MX by focusing on these 10 FANtastic plays. What's your next move to bring home the win?

THE BALL IS IN YOUR COURT—PRACTICE DRILL #9

Conduct a deep dive into your website's analytic reports. If you don't know how to interpret them, hire an expert to help you. Become familiar with your performance numbers. Set up automated reporting so that you receive the reports at least once a month. Take the time to review your reports or delegate this task to someone on your team.

Takeaway For Marketers: Your website isn't just a digital placeholder—it's your hardest-working player on the field, driving leads and creating first impressions 24/7. To WOW your audience and convert visitors into loyal fans, it must be more than visually appealing; it must also be strategic, functional, and up to date. A website that is clear, fast, easy to navigate, and packed with social proof ensures your business stays ahead of the competition.

Secret #5

GET OFF THE SIDELINES

Score Big by Owning Your Digital Turf

IMAGINE THIS: the star quarterback of a championship team sitting idle on the sidelines during the season's biggest game. Sounds ridiculous, right? In marketing, allowing your brand to be invisible while your competitors dominate the digital playing field is unthinkable. Heavy hitters like Coke, Nike, Disney, and Target don't just sit on the sidelines—they control the game, ensuring their messaging is seen, heard, and remembered. They're not just playing the game; they own the field.

These brands employ every tactic in the marketing playbook to capture attention. Consider Coke: you might see a Coke ad on YouTube, pass a Coke billboard during your commute, notice a tweet sponsored by Coke, and grab a bottle featuring a QR code that links to a Coke contest. This omnipresence establishes Coke as the MVP of consumer memory—it's no coincidence that they're always at the *top of people's minds*. Coke doesn't just make plays; they score touchdowns.

BUT WHAT ABOUT THE REST OF US?

These brands have Super Bowl-sized budgets, but don't count yourself out yet. Even if your marketing budget doesn't compare to that of a major league team, you can still make strategic moves to help you stand out. Using affordable, high-impact strategies, a smaller brand can still score because of the power of digital marketing.

Consider the story of **Saddleback Leather Company**™. It's a small business with a significant online presence. Here's how they advanced their efforts.

I became acquainted with the Saddleback Leather Company when my dad, a retired Senior HR Leader and Executive Coach who has a passion for quality leather goods, found Saddleback Leather online. The company's tagline, **"They'll fight over it when you're dead,"** caught his eye and amused him. Their rugged, handcrafted products appealed to his VALS-driven Principles and Values buying motivation. However, the $600 price tag on a briefcase gave him pause. So, he didn't buy it at first.

That's when Saddleback initiated their version of the two-minute drill. My dad kept encountering their retargeting banner ads across the web—on Facebook, news sites, and even in his email inbox. They didn't sit back and hope he'd return; they followed up, nudging him just enough to keep their product in his mind. Before long, he made the purchase—a testament to the power of persistent, targeted digital marketing. When he called to tell me he made the purchase, he enthusiastically and humorously said, "You and your brother can fight over it when I'm dead."

Saddleback isn't playing around. Its digital footprint includes a stunning website, engaging videos, a compelling company backstory and mission, a blog packed with stories, and an active presence on Google, Facebook, Instagram, and more. Saddleback has perfected the art of turning curious visitors into lifelong fans.

AVOID THE WITNESS PROTECTION PROGRAM

Does your business feel like it's in the online version of the witness protection program? If you're challenging to find online, you might as well not exist. Try Googling your industry and product category(s) with your location(s). If you don't appear on the first or second page of the search results, you're invisible to potential fans. The same goes for social media. If you're not active on platforms like Instagram, Pinterest, or Facebook—or worse, if your online reviews are filled with complaints you've ignored—you're stuck on the sidelines, missing out on the action.

Business growth depends not on who you know, but on who knows YOU.

Retail business owners understand the significance of a great location in the physical world. Consider your digital presence as your *online storefront*. The prime real estate? High-traffic platforms such as search engines and social media sites. You must secure your place in these digital hotspots and establish a consistent presence to stay competitive.

MEREDITH'S WAGON WHEEL OF MARKETING

Picture your marketing strategy as a wagon wheel. The hub of the wheel is your website—your home base, your quarterback, where everything connects. Your traffic drivers are the spokes on the wheel: SEO, email marketing, social media ads, and more (see below for an exhaustive list). The wheel rim is your audience, waiting to be drawn in. To win the game, your spokes must be strong and diverse, bringing visitors to your hub from all directions.

Many years ago, during the dot-com boom, I worked for a startup online directory selling online advertising. My boss, John Nethero, was well-known for saying, "A website without web marketing is like a billboard in the Everglades. It doesn't exist." Over twenty years later, I've never forgotten this principle. He was right. You may have a FANtastic website and truly understand your audience, but if no one knows about your business, it doesn't matter.

Let's expand your playbook. Here are traffic drivers you can add to your strategy:

Digital Traffic Drivers

✔ Affiliate Marketing
✔ Chatbots
✔ Content Marketing
✔ Display Ads
✔ Email Marketing

- ✔ Gamification
- ✔ Influencer Collaborations
- ✔ Interactive Content
- ✔ Loyalty Programs
- ✔ Mobile App Advertising
- ✔ Online Community Engagement
- ✔ Online Directories
- ✔ Online Partnerships and Sponsorships
- ✔ Paid Search Marketing (SEM)
- ✔ Podcasting
- ✔ Popups
- ✔ Press Releases
- ✔ Search Engine Optimization (SEO)
- ✔ Social Media Marketing
- ✔ Video Marketing and Ads
- ✔ Virtual Events and Webinars

Offline Traffic Drivers

- ✔ Billboards and Signage
- ✔ Broadcast Media (TV, radio)
- ✔ Brochures and Flyers
- ✔ Business Cards
- ✔ Charity Sponsorships
- ✔ Collabs with Local Businesses
- ✔ Custom Packaging
- ✔ Direct Mail
- ✔ Editorial Print Stories
- ✔ Event Sponsorships
- ✔ Events and Tradeshows
- ✔ In-Store Events

- ✔ Labels and Inserts
- ✔ Local Meetups
- ✔ Loyalty Programs
- ✔ Networking Events
- ✔ Point-of-Sale Displays
- ✔ Print Ads
- ✔ Promotional Items and Merch
- ✔ Receipts and Invoices
- ✔ Referral Groups
- ✔ Stickers and Decals
- ✔ Telephone and Voicemail Messages
- ✔ Trade Associations
- ✔ Vehicle Advertising
- ✔ Word-of-Mouth Referrals
- ✔ Workshops and Seminars

Both lists are quite extensive. Don't get overwhelmed. You shouldn't and don't need to use every tactic, but a winning strategy combines a mix of these drivers.

HOW DO YOU KNOW WHICH TRAFFIC DRIVERS TO SELECT?

If I had a magic playbook with a guaranteed, one-size-fits-all formula for selecting the perfect marketing mix, I'd share it with you in a heartbeat. But you already know the answer—it all depends on your fans! This is why implementing Secret #3 is so important. While I can't make the decisions for your team without data and deeper insight into your business, I *can* help you create a playbook with the right questions and steps.

Step #1—Interview Your Fans: Understand the Game Plan

Your last 25 customers are like your star players—they understand how the game unfolds. Send out surveys, conduct focus groups, and one-on-one interviews to map their buying journey. Ask them questions like:

- How did you first hear about our business?
- How much time passed before you did further research?
- What channels did you use to research our product, service, or brand?
- Which channels do you usually avoid or would never use to learn about us?

Step #2—Use Google Analytics 4: Scout the Stats

Think of GA4 as your assistant coach—it provides the complex data that tells you where to focus your energy. Log into your account, open the **Reporting tab**, click **Acquisition**, and select **Traffic Acquisition**. This report shows the top traffic sources to your website. Expand the table to uncover additional sources (up to 250 if needed!). See Secret #9 for an in-depth review of GA4.

If you don't see major players like Google or Facebook in your traffic report, it's time to boost your presence on these platforms. And if your existing channels (spokes on your wagon wheel) do not appear on the report, you've identified opportunities to fix tracking issues or switch up your strategy.

Step #3—Ask the Right Questions: Build a Playbook Around Your Goals

Marketing success depends on aligning your tactics with your business goals and capabilities.

To refine your strategy, answer these critical questions:

- What's your overall marketing goal? Brand awareness? Lead generation? Immediate sales?
- What's your annual marketing budget? Can it be reallocated to better-performing strategies?
- Do you need a short-term game plan to deliver fast results or a long-term strategy to build your brand?
- Who will manage your web marketing efforts, and what's their experience level?
- Is your website compelling and up to date? How many leads does it currently generate?
- How will you evaluate the success of your marketing campaigns?
- What tactics are your competitors using effectively?
- Can some or all of your marketing be outsourced?
- Who will make the final decisions and implement your plan?

Your answers will help you draft a playbook that fits your unique goals, budget, and audience.

Short-Term Tactics—Quick Wins for the Highlight Reel

You must first decide whether you need *immediate* results to drive traffic or a *medium to long-term approach*. These strategies are like fast-break plays—quick and effective:

- ✔ Billboards and Signage
- ✔ Broadcast Media (TV, radio)
- ✔ Display Ads
- ✔ Email Marketing
- ✔ Influencer Collaborations
- ✔ Sponsored Interactive Content (Quizzes and Polls)
- ✔ Mobile App Advertising
- ✔ Online Directories
- ✔ Paid Search Marketing (SEM)
- ✔ Popups
- ✔ Press Releases
- ✔ Social Media Ads
- ✔ Video Marketing and Ads
- ✔ Virtual Events and Webinars

Long-Term Tactics—Building a Legacy Team

If you're focused on building your brand and creating sustainable growth, these *medium to long-term* approaches are your championship strategy:

- ✔ Affiliate Marketing
- ✔ Broadcast Media (TV, radio)
- ✔ Brochures and Flyers
- ✔ Business Cards
- ✔ Charity Sponsorships
- ✔ Chatbots

- ✔ Collabs with Local Businesses
- ✔ Content Marketing
- ✔ Custom Packaging
- ✔ Custom Packaging
- ✔ Editorial Print Stories
- ✔ Event Sponsorships
- ✔ Events and Tradeshows
- ✔ Gamification
- ✔ In-Store Events
- ✔ Influencer Collaborations
- ✔ Interactive Content (Quizzes and Polls)
- ✔ Labels and Inserts
- ✔ Local Meetups
- ✔ Loyalty Programs
- ✔ Networking Events
- ✔ Online Community Engagement
- ✔ Online Directories
- ✔ Online Partnerships and Sponsorships
- ✔ Podcasting
- ✔ Point-of-Sale Displays
- ✔ Popups
- ✔ Press Releases
- ✔ Promotional Items and Merch
- ✔ Receipts and Invoices
- ✔ Referral Groups
- ✔ Search Engine Optimization (SEO)
- ✔ Social Media Marketing
- ✔ Stickers and Decals
- ✔ Telephone and Voicemail Messages
- ✔ Trade Associations
- ✔ Vehicle Advertising

- ✔ Virtual Events and Webinars
- ✔ Word-of-Mouth Referrals
- ✔ Workshops and Seminars

GAME PLAN—HOW TO START

Every successful team begins with a solid game plan, and developing your marketing strategy is no different. Whether launching a new campaign or fine-tuning an existing one, these **seven key steps** will guide you from preparation to execution, keeping you focused, strategic, and ready to win.

1. **Scout the Field**—Identify and profile your target market—your most valuable players.

2. **Invest in the Hub**—Build the best website you can afford—it's the hub of your marketing wheel and your franchise quarterback.

3. **Pick Your Plays**—Choose two or three traffic drivers (like spokes on a wheel) to begin. It's best to use both online and offline traffic drivers.

4. **Set the Schedule**—Outline your promotions and timing.

5. **Measure Success**—Track your first campaign's performance. See Secret #9 for how to do this with GA4.

6. **Tweak and Refine**—Adjust your strategy based on data and feedback.

7. **Repeat**—Keep refining your game plan as you go.

WHEN TO CALL IN THE PROS

If you've followed these steps and still can't pinpoint the right mix of traffic drivers, it might be time to call in a consultant or marketing agency. A seasoned coach can help analyze your business, share case studies, and recommend proven plays that work for businesses like yours.

Focusing on your fans and aligning your strategies with their needs will help you create a winning strategy for monopolizing your digital space.

THE BALL IS IN YOUR COURT—PRACTICE DRILL #10

Draw a wagon wheel on a clean sheet of paper. Based on the findings from Steps #1 - #3 above, label the wheel's spokes with your current traffic drivers. Then, create a second wheel with new online and offline traffic drivers you plan to implement.

Takeaway for Marketers: Building a successful marketing strategy is dynamic and ongoing, like adjusting your game plan at halftime. Your updated wagon wheel symbolizes your evolving playbook, merging proven tactics with fresh ideas to drive traffic and engagement. By identifying the spokes that work and incorporating new, targeted drivers, you'll develop a robust, multi-channel strategy designed to meet your fans where they are and guide them to your hub. Remember: staying proactive and adaptable keeps you in the game and ahead of the competition.

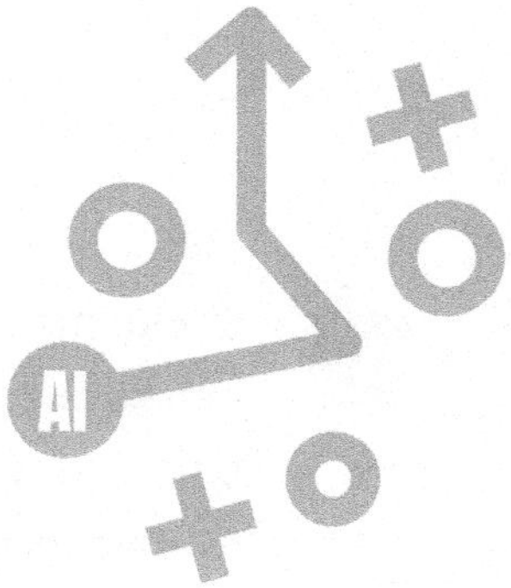

Secret #6
MOVE THE GOALPOSTS

Supersize Your Social Media

I HAVE AN EMBARRASSING secret to confess about social media marketing. My personal use of social media was slow to join the conversation. I once told a digital marketing colleague that social media was a fad and wouldn't endure because I believed others weren't interested in the mundane details of our lives. Woof.

Now that you've stopped laughing at my naiveté rest assured that I've been fully committed to social media marketing for many years. I do recognize and remain concerned about its negative impacts, especially on our youth. Limiting social media access for young people is a critical imperative, and society must unite to make social media safer for them.

Social media marketing is one of the best digital marketing tools for leveling the playing field, particularly for entrepreneurs, influencers, freelancers, and small businesses.

In football, the goalposts stay put. Marketing, however, demands a different approach. In today's ever-evolving digital landscape, you must move your marketing goalposts. Set new, dynamic targets that adapt to change. This might come quickly for some, as you're new to marketing and have yet to settle into habits. For others, this shift might feel as disorienting as it would for a quarterback whose end zone suddenly relocates mid-play.

WHY SOCIAL MEDIA MARKETING IS A MUST-HAVE

The social media scene has grown beyond platforms like Facebook, Instagram, and YouTube. With newer contenders like TikTok, Threads®, and BeReal® capturing user attention, businesses must remain adaptable to where audiences spend their time. **According to Pew Research, most Americans—approximately 72%—engage with social media daily.**[40]

Here's why you can't afford to ignore it:

1. **Broad Reach**—Platforms such as TikTok, Instagram Reels, and YouTube Shorts enable your brand to engage with younger audiences, whereas Facebook continues to be a mainstay for Gen X and Boomers.

2. **Word-of-Tap and Social Proof**—In addition to *word-of-mouse*, today's world thrives on user-generated content (UGC), including unboxing videos, TikTok reviews, and live-streamed experiences.

3. **Reviews and Validation**—Google Business Profiles, Yelp®, and platforms like Trustpilot® highlight the significance of reviews. Positive feedback across these channels is essential for building trust.

Effective social media marketing requires more than simple observation and reportage. Instead, it demands creative thinking and consistent application of recognized principles in public relations. In companies and offices where much of the staff already have their hands full with routine tasks, there's simply no one available to craft clever Facebook, Instagram, and X posts to make customers flock to the products. But here's the problem: You don't have a choice. Effective social media use is a required move for businesses today.

Tip #1—Stop the Vanity Post Madness

Avoid turning your social media into a self-serving mirror. Users see through your vanity posts, making your brand seem tone-deaf or out of touch. For example, in the age of cultural and social awareness, pausing pre-scheduled posts during moments of national or global tragedy is critical—tone and timing matter.

Take a cue from Samsung's infamous "What's the one device you'd take to a deserted island?" campaign that **unintentionally generated hundreds of comments mentioning the iPhone** instead of Samsung® devices. Instead of seeking empty praise, focus on genuine engagement.

Connecting to Fan DNA

- ✔ **Self-Esteem**—Fans want to feel proud of the brands they support. Instead of posting content purely for applause, share stories of customer success, meaningful brand contributions, or community involvement. These moments give fans something to rally behind and feel proud of.

- ✔ **State Change**—Great content can shift moods, inspire action, or even provide relief. Avoid posts that feel disconnected or self-congratulatory. Instead, focus on content that entertains, educates, or emotionally resonates with your audience.

Tip #2 – Show the Real You

Your audience craves authenticity. Take, for instance, the annual Epcot® International Food & Wine Festival, one of the theme park's most popular and heavily attended events. Fans cherish it so much that Disney's marketing team provides an inside look at festival preparations through blog posts, TikToks, and Instagram Lives. This marketing content highlights impressive statistics of the event—over 900,000 dishes served and 338,000 glasses of wine poured—while adding a personal touch by showcasing the behind-the-scenes efforts of cast members, thus strengthening fandom and fan relationships.

Connecting to Fan DNA

- ✔ **Identity**—Disney has a dedicated fanbase that invests thousands in yearly vacations, proudly sports Disney merchandise, and commemorates life's milestones at its parks. These fans, closely bonded through treasured memories, experience a sense of belonging and perceive Disney as an extension of their family.

Behind-the-scenes content and the powerful Disney brand enhance the shared identity of millions of fans worldwide.

- ✔ **Sense of Belonging**—Disney employees are known as Cast Members, while theme park visitors are referred to as Guests. Bestowing warm titles and highlighting the behind-the-scenes human aspect of Disney fosters an emotional bond between Cast Members and Guests, inviting them into the community.

Tip #3—Master the Art of the Shout-Out

Fan recognition fosters loyalty. Wendy's exemplifies this through their annual National Roast Day, during which fans invite the brand to roast them on X. This campaign transforms passive followers into active participants, generating millions of impressions. Wendy's also engages with fans' posts, responding with humor or validation, thereby establishing a strong emotional connection with their audience.

Connecting to Fan DNA

- ✔ **Self-Esteem**—Acknowledging fans' contributions makes them feel seen, valued, and appreciated, boosting their confidence.

- ✔ **Sense of Belonging**—By engaging directly, you create a community where fans feel vital to your brand's culture.

Tip #4—Write Like You Talk

High-engagement social media posts sound human. Your audience doesn't want to read corporate jargon; they want to feel engaged with a real person. Use conversational language, emojis (when appropriate), and short sentences to make your posts relatable. For example, Wendy's quick, snappy tweets and TikTok quips feel like they come from a friend, not a brand. This approach builds rapport and encourages interaction.

Connecting to Fan DNA

- ✔ **State Change**—Conversational, engaging posts can shift fans' moods, making them laugh, smile, or feel more connected during their day.

- ✔ **Escapism**—Casual, fun language frees fans from the monotony of formal communication or stressful news cycles.

Tip #5—Emphasize Visuals

Visual content drives higher engagement than text alone. **According to HubSpot, tweets with images get 150% more retweets, and Instagram posts with video generate 49% more engagement than those with static images.** Short-form video reigns supreme among visuals, with TikTok, Reels, and YouTube Shorts seeing the highest interaction rates. For example, Oreo's TikTok challenges, featuring playful snack hacks and recipes, have made their brand iconic with younger audiences.

To maximize engagement:

- ✔ Use *authentic* visuals, including team photos, behind-the-scenes videos, and user-generated content. Ensure any stock photos *represent your audience* and adhere to regulations like the Fair Housing Act in the real estate industry.

- ✔ Invest in infographics to communicate data or processes. Studies show that infographics increase engagement by up to 80%.[41]

✔ Optimize for mobile. Vertical videos and photos perform better on platforms like TikTok and Instagram.

Connecting to Fan DNA

✔ **Escapism**—Vibrant visuals and dynamic videos allow fans to immerse themselves in something uplifting and entertaining.

✔ **State Change**—Eye-catching visuals can elevate fans' emotions, creating excitement and making your brand.

By directly linking these actionable tips to the 5 DNA Traits of a Fan—Identity, Self-Esteem, Escapism, State Change, and Sense of Belonging—you can develop a social media strategy that resonates deeply on an emotional level. These traits provide the foundation for converting followers into fiercely loyal advocates for your brand.

THE BALL IS IN YOUR COURT—PRACTICE DRILL #11

Brainstorm with your team to identify creative, engaging content that humanizes your brand, highlights key partnerships, and showcases compelling visuals:

1. **Behind-the-Scenes Content**—Develop a list of behind-the-scenes moments to share on social media. Show how your products are made, introduce team members, or provide a sneak peek into your daily operations. Draw inspiration from brands like Disney, which excels at storytelling and self-revelation.

2. **Recognize VIPs**—Identify your Very Important Partners (VIPs), including vendors, collaborators, referrers, and community organizations. Create posts that spotlight their contributions and celebrate their impact on your business. Publicly acknowledging these relationships fosters goodwill and strengthens your brand community.

3. **Plan Visual Assets**—Evaluate your need for visuals, such as product photos, testimonial videos, or event footage. Create a plan to consistently capture high-quality images and videos at key moments in your workflow. Organize these assets in a cloud-based library for easy access and ensure your team has a clear strategy for incorporating them into your marketing.

Takeaway for Marketers: Engaging content is grounded in authenticity, collaboration, and visual appeal. By showcasing your brand's humanity, celebrating partnerships, and utilizing powerful visuals, you can cultivate a relatable and memorable presence that enhances connections with your audience.

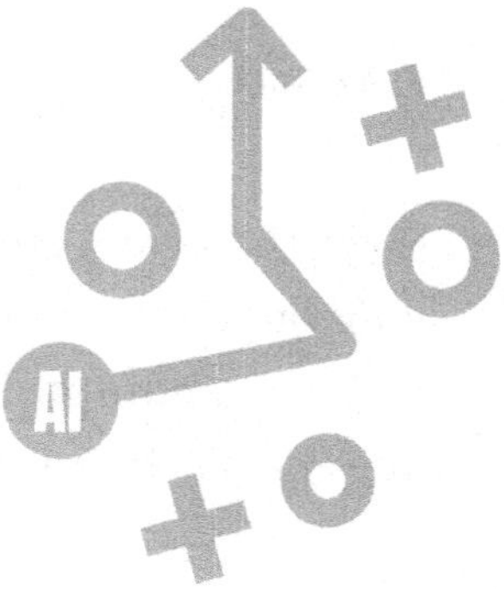

Secret #7

GO THE DISTANCE

AI-Accelerated Content Marketing

CONTENT MARKETING IS a forceful strategy that extends beyond quick interactions on social media. It fosters lasting relationships by providing consistent, valuable, relevant content that resonates with your audience's needs. While social media serves as the platform for engagement, content marketing establishes a foundation of trust, authority, and loyalty, offering substance that remains with your audience long after the likes and shares fade.

Content marketing thrives on its adaptability. In today's world, the variety of content formats has expanded dramatically, giving brands more ways than ever to connect with their audiences.

Content marketing goes beyond a sales pitch and allows you to interact with your fans more meaningfully.

Over the years, content marketing has emerged as a reliable and consistent force among digital marketing tactics. Thus, it is valuable to have a comprehensive list to consult when deciding which approach is best for your business.

- **Blog Posts**—Blogs remain a cornerstone of content marketing. However, longer-form content (1,500—2,500 words) optimized for SEO is now standard. Incorporate expert interviews, data insights, and case studies to provide readers with actionable information.

- **Short-Form Video**—Platforms like TikTok, Instagram Reels, and YouTube Shorts are perfect for quick, engaging storytelling. Use these formats to showcase products, share behind-the-scenes moments, or deliver 60-second educational content tips.

- **Interactive Content**—Quizzes, calculators, and augmented reality (AR) experiences are gaining popularity. AR allows users to visualize furniture in their homes or experiment with makeup shades before purchasing.

- **Infographics**—Infographics are a powerful way to communicate complex ideas quickly. Design them to align with your brand's aesthetic and share them on your website and social media platforms.

- **Memes**—While memes remain enjoyable and shareable, incorporating branded humor that resonates with your audience's interests can make your content more likely to go viral.

- **Long-Form Video and Webinars**—Beyond quick videos, in-depth live webinars or YouTube series are ideal for audiences who want to delve deeper. Consider product tutorials, expert interviews, or panel discussions.

- **Podcasts**—Podcasts are an excellent way to build thought leadership and engage listeners during commutes or workouts. To keep your episodes relevant, feature guests and highlight industry trends.

- **Whitepapers, E-Books, and Guides**—These content types are highly effective for generating leads. Ensure they provide valuable insights and practical advice tailored to your audience's challenges.

- **Purpose-Driven Campaigns**—Today's consumers are drawn to brands that reflect their values. Share content highlighting your sustainability efforts, inclusivity initiatives, or partnerships with charitable endeavors.

USING AI IN CONTENT CREATION

AI is transforming the content creation landscape, making brainstorming, writing, designing, and optimizing faster and easier. But here's the key point—AI is only as effective as how you use it.

It's not about replacing creativity; it's about enhancing it. Whether you're drafting blog posts, creating visuals, or planning campaigns, these tips will help you collaborate with AI to produce authentic, on-brand, and impactful content. Typically, I would include two additional tips in the list below. However, we've covered them in **Secret #2**: 1) Use AI for Idea Generation (Brainstorming), and 2) Combine HI with AI.

With that in mind, let's break it down!

Tip #1—Start with Clear and Detailed Prompts

AI tools like ChatGPT and Jasper thrive on specific instructions. Instead of asking:

- "Write a blog about marketing," consider saying,
- "Create a 1,000-word blog post on how a locally owned coffee shop in Raleigh, NC, can utilize content marketing to boost sales of cold coffee drinks during the summer, including examples of best practices."
- This approach helps the AI grasp your objectives and provides focused results.

Tip #2—Train AI on Your Brand Voice

Many AI tools can be customized to reflect your brand's tone and style. Opt for the paid version of the ChatGPT to create a custom GPT (ask ChatGPT for a step-by-step guide on how to set one up—it's simple once you have the instructions). A custom GPT adapts to your style and content faster than the free version. Upload relevant documents about your brand to the custom GPT documents section, including:

- Brand guide
- Brochures and flyers
- CVs and bios of company team members
- Lists of awards and affiliations
- Podcast and webinar recording sample

- Portfolio of past, completed products or service
- PowerPoint or Keynote slide decks
- Samples of blog posts, social media posts, and mass email campaigns
- Website address

Tip #3—Incorporate Generative AI into Campaign Strategy

AI platforms can go beyond content creation to propose whole campaign strategies. For example, you can input your objectives and receive a recommended campaign framework that includes blog topics, social media posts, and ad copy. Moreover, you can request that AI identify content gaps in your current strategy and suggest exploring new areas.

Tip #4—Create Personalized Content

AI excels at analyzing user data to create content that genuinely engages diverse audiences. For instance, tools like HubSpot® can automatically generate personalized email messages that thoughtfully reflect user behavior. Moreover, AI-powered chatbots are excellent at recommending products or answering frequently asked questions, enhancing the experience to feel tailored to each user.

Tip #5—Repurpose Existing Content

AI excels at transforming content into various formats. For example,

- Convert blogs into scripts for short videos using tools like Synthesia®.
- Summarize webinars into social media posts or infographics with Canva.

- Create concise key takeaways from lengthy eBooks for email marketing campaigns.

- Condense long-form video content into 1–2-minute social media clips with Munch®.

- Use Otter.ai® to generate a transcript of webinars and then leverage ChatGPT and Grammarly to craft a blog post based on the transcript.

Tip #6—Develop Content Frameworks

Use AI to build detailed frameworks for recurring content types. For example, develop a standard template for:

- Blog posts, including headings, subheadings, and CTA placements.

- Social media campaigns, specifying tone, hashtags, and key messages.

- Webinars or podcast outlines highlighting key discussion points.

Tip #7—Refine Your Writing

AI can polish drafts, improve tone, and optimize readability. Tools like Grammarly or Hemingway® can refine grammar, while ChatGPT can adjust tone. Example:

- Original—"We sell software to help businesses grow."

- AI Refinement—"Our software empowers home services companies to scale efficiently and achieve their growth goals."

Tip #8—Experiment with Interactive AI Content

AI-generated interactive content, including quizzes, calculators, and augmented reality experiences, enhances engagement by directly involving users. For example:

- Create a quiz powered by AI that recommends products based on user input preferences.

- Leverage AR tools to allow customers to visualize products in their environments, such as furniture or paint colors.

Tip #9—Leverage AI for Visuals

AI tools can assist you in incorporating eye-catching visuals. For instance, you can utilize Canva for branded infographics or carousel posts. DALL·E or MidJourney™ can create unique artwork based on your text prompts. Adobe Firefly® lets you enhance existing designs with AI-driven effects.

Tip #10—Automate Content Scheduling and Distribution

Save time by automating repetitive tasks with tools like Hootsuite Amplify™ or Buffer®. These tools use AI to optimize posting schedules for maximum engagement. You can also use Zapier to set up workflows that automatically publish content across multiple platforms.

Tip #11—Enhance Video Content with AI

AI tools such as Synthesia® enable you to create professional videos without the need for costly equipment or actors. You can use virtual avatars to deliver tutorials or product overviews. Similarly, tools like Pictory® can convert long-form text into captivating video summaries, repurposing your content for video-first platforms.

Tip #12—Optimize Content for Voice Search

As voice search becomes more prevalent, adapt your content for conversational queries. Use AI to analyze commonly spoken questions and optimize your content to match. To capture voice search traffic, focus on natural language, question-based formats, and featured snippets.

SMART CONTENT ROCKS

In today's crowded digital landscape, **Smart Content** is not merely a luxury; it is essential for capturing attention, fostering meaningful connections, and driving results.

What makes content smart?
It's not only about quality; it's about purpose.

To create smart content, follow these best practices:

- Design for your ideal fan using the language they understand.
- Provide education, inspiration, or entertainment—addressing key questions and solving challenges.
- Stay consistent. Maintain a content calendar for posting regularly.
- Encourage sharing, whether through integrated social buttons or content that has the potential to go viral material.
- Always connect back to your brand, subtly highlighting your expertise and products.

- Include a strong call to action demonstrating the value fans will gain by engaging.
- Ensure measurability. Use tools like HubSpot, SEMrush, or advanced Google Analytics to track metrics such as time spent on the site, social shares, and conversion rates.

A straightforward way to integrate content marketing development into your daily routine is to think like a journalist. Stay alert for opportunities to capture photos and video material. Look for chances to interact with fans and ask them questions relevant to your business and answer the most frequently asked questions from your current fans. The key to creating impactful content marketing is to provide value by explaining why the content matters. To establish yourself as an expert, go beyond mere reporting. It's the in-depth analysis that sets you apart.

Success in content marketing isn't merely about producing more—it's about making better. The most effective content captures attention, delivers value, and keeps your audience engaged from beginning to end. Below are three key principles to guide your strategy and ensure your content stands out in a crowded digital landscape.

1. **Show, Don't Tell**—Follow classic storytelling principles for a more effective response. Demonstrating your message with visuals is more impactful than conveying it through text alone. Press releases with multiple images receive six times more engagement than text-only releases.[42] Blog posts featuring videos attract 83% more traffic than those without.[43]

2. **Design for Scanning, Not Reading**—On average, users read at most **28%** of the words on a webpage; realistically, it's closer

to **20%**. The average visit to a webpage lasts less than a minute, with many under 10 seconds. **97% of users read headlines and sub-headlines** and usually scan pages in an *F-shaped pattern*.[44] At Meredith Communications, we always say that you *write* copy and blogs for Google search bots (SEO) and design *visuals* for your fans. Use short paragraphs, clear headings, and bullet points. Place crucial details in high-visibility zones, like the upper-left corner or bolded text.

3. **Organize Your Post**—Your audience shouldn't have to work hard to understand your message. If your main point is buried deep in the text or hidden behind unnecessary details, you risk losing their attention before they reach it. State your case or make your primary point **early in the copy**—ideally in the headline, first sentence, or opening paragraph. Use the *inverted pyramid structure*, placing the most critical information at the top and supporting details below. Break up large blocks of text with **clear subheadings, bullet points, and bolded phrases** to make your content scannable. Remember: *every paragraph should add value.* Avoid filler content, overly long introductions, or tangents that might distract your audience from your main message.

By presenting your information in a **logical, easy-to-follow structure**, you'll keep your readers engaged and ensure your message sticks.

EXAMPLES OF CONTENT MARKETING EXCELLENCE

Case Study: Glossier®

Beauty brand Glossier has perfected the art of user-generated content (UGC). By encouraging customers to post photos and reviews on social media, Glossier enhances its brand voice while fostering authenticity. Their content showcases real fans using their products, which resonates much more than traditional advertising.

Spotlight: Duolingo®
Duolingo's humor and relatability on TikTok have transformed how brands engage with younger audiences. Their quirky mascot, Duo the Owl, appears in amusing, trending videos that keep fans entertained while subtly promoting their language-learning app.

Event Campaign: Patagonia®
Patagonia's content extends beyond merely selling apparel. Its campaigns emphasize sustainability and environmental activism. By sharing interactive infographics, in-depth articles, and brief videos about climate change, Patagonia establishes itself as a trusted brand and a thought leader.

THE GOALPOSTS OF MODERN CONTENT MARKETING

Set clear objectives from the beginning: Are you aiming to educate, entertain, or inspire? Do you want to grow your email list, increase traffic, or improve conversions? Once your goals are defined, you can choose the right content mix to achieve them. For example:

- To educate, concentrate on long-form blogs, tutorials, or webinars.
- To entertain, short-form videos and memes are most effective.
- To inspire, utilize storytelling through testimonials, case studies, or purpose-driven campaigns.
- To generate more leads, focus on providing valuable resources in exchange for contact information. Create downloadable guides,

whitepapers, or exclusive webinars and place them behind lead capture forms. Combine these with compelling calls-to-action (CTAs) and strategically positioned sign-up forms throughout your website and content.

Content marketing isn't just about publishing—it's about delivering value. Whether through educational e-books, engaging videos, or community-driven campaigns, your content should consistently reflect your brand's identity. Follow these principles; your content will earn your fan's trust and loyalty.

THE BALL IS IN YOUR COURT—PRACTICE DRILL #12

Compile a comprehensive list of the questions most frequently asked by your fans. Include every question; none is too small or unimportant—list as many as possible. Afterward, review the list to eliminate duplicates. Organize the questions into categories by topic. Create a master FAQ document using Excel, Sheets, or Google Docs. When seeking inspiration for your content marketing, start with the questions on the list.

Takeaway For Marketers: Your fans' questions offer invaluable insights into their needs, concerns, and desires. Organizing these questions into a comprehensive FAQ establishes a roadmap for creating content that truly resonates. Whether it's a blog post, social media update, video tutorial, or podcast topic, addressing these inquiries positions your brand as a trusted authority while connecting with your fans where they are.

Part IV

CHARGE THE BACK NINE

"To me, life is like the back nine in golf.
Sometimes, you get better on the back nine.
You may not be stronger, but hopefully, you are wiser."

Clint Eastwood, American Film Actor, Producer, Director and Composer
Four-Time Academy Award Winner

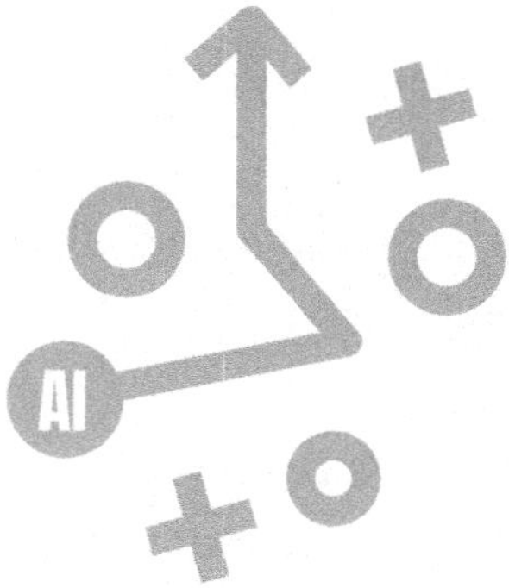

Secret #8

KEEP THE BALL ROLLING

Mastering Your Online Reputation

IN THE REALM of FANtastic Marketing, maintaining momentum is everything. Whether you're skating on the ice, driving down the fairway, or rallying on the tennis court, safeguarding your online reputation is like playing a high-stakes championship match. Every review, comment, and interaction impacts your overall score. Let's lace up, tee off, or get into our ready stance—your reputation game begins now.

Online reputation is dynamic and ever-changing, shaped by what customers say about your brand.

Online reviews have become a cornerstone of consumer decision-making:

- **Prevalence of Review Reading**—Over **99% of American consumers** read online reviews before purchasing.[45]

- **Trust in Reviews**—Approximately **84% of consumers** trust online reviews as much as personal recommendations, which rises to **91%** among 18- to 34-year-olds.[46]

- **Impact on Revenue**—A **one-star increase** in a Yelp rating can lead to a **5-9%** increase in revenue, underscoring the financial impact of online reputation.[47]

- **More Reviews are Better**—**59% of consumers** expect a business to have between **20-99 reviews** to trust the average star rating.[48]

Brian Solis, the author of *The End of Business as Usual*, said, "Your brand is defined not by advertisers but by those who experience it." This truth has only deepened with time. Customers trust reviews from others like themselves more than any corporate promise. Google's ZMOT Research (Zero Moment of Truth) emphasizes that potential buyers research extensively before making decisions. Your reviews are a key part of this journey, acting as your silent salespeople, either building your credibility or eroding it.

IF WE IGNORE ONLINE REVIEWS, THEY DON'T EXIST

Oh, how I wish that were true! When I speak to business owners and marketing leaders, I repeatedly hear the same fears about online reviews. Do any of these fears sound familiar?

- If we engage with a negative review, it will exacerbate the situation and make it worse.

- If we build a presence on a review site like Yelp, it will only attract negative reviews.

- We will never make everyone happy, and only unhappy customers post reviews.

Most businesses fail to manage online reviews because they feel they are pushing a boulder uphill and/or lack a process with assigned task accountability. Receiving a harmful or completely fraudulent review is frustrating and disheartening, and it makes marketers want to throw their hands up in frustration.

I have good news for you. While having a perfect 5.0 review average is a worthy goal, studies show it's unnecessary and can be counterproductive. Say what?! **82% of shoppers actively seek out negative reviews to gauge credibility, as overly polished, five-star ratings are often viewed skeptically.**[49] Consumers tend to trust brands more when they see a mix of feedback, which suggests authenticity and transparency. A near-perfect score with a few constructive criticisms demonstrates your reviews are genuine. It allows you to showcase how you handle less-than-ideal experiences—ultimately building trust with prospective customers.

The perfect online star rating *for perception purposes* is typically between 4.2 and 4.7 stars.

This range strikes the ideal balance between demonstrating high-quality service or products while appearing authentic and credible. Conversely, ratings below 4.0 can raise red flags about consistent issues with quality or service. A 4.2-4.7 average suggests your business delivers exceptional experiences while being real enough to acknowledge occasional imperfections, which reassures customers and fosters trust.

THE GOOGLE BUSINESS PROFILE (GBP) ADVANTAGE

If you haven't already, the first place to start building up good reviews is on your **GBP.** It is indispensable for managing your online reputation. **81% of consumers use Google to read reviews and evaluate local businesses.**[50] It is often the first impression customers have of your business. Here's how to maximize its potential:

Step #1—Claim and Optimize Your GBP Profile

Ensure your business information—name, address, phone, and hours—is accurate and up-to-date.

✓ **Why It Matters:** Profiles act as your digital storefront. An incomplete or inaccurate profile can drive customers away, while a well-maintained profile boosts your local and map search visibility.

✓ **What to Do:**

- Conduct an audit for each location listed in your GBP account.
- Update NAP (Name, Address, Phone), office hours, and parking information consistently across profiles.
- Regularly add high-quality photos and videos showcasing your products, services, team, or store environment.

- Monitor daily for new reviews. Respond to all reviews. See below for detailed best practices on how to respond.

Pro Tip: Use UTM tracking links in your GBP profile to monitor how much traffic or leads it generates via Google Analytics.

Step #2—Encourage Customer Reviews

Know that timing is key. Ask immediately after a successful interaction when the experience is fresh in the customer's mind. For example: "Thank you for visiting/buying from us today! Your feedback would mean the world to us. Could you leave us a review here: [Insert Link]."

Place QR codes on physical receipts, brochures, or in-store signage that link directly to your review page. For example: "Loved your visit? Scan this code to share your experience!"

Use tools like Birdeye or Reputation.com to send automated emails or SMS messages post-transaction. For Example:

✔ **First Email:** "Hi [Customer Name], thank you for choosing [Business Name]! If you had a great experience, we'd love for you to share it. [Insert Link]."

✔ **Follow-Up Email (if no review):** "We noticed you didn't get a chance to leave feedback. Your input helps us improve!"

Step #3—Respond to All Reviews

Respond to positive and negative reviews. For example, "Thank you for your glowing review, [Customer Name]! We're thrilled to hear that [specific service/product] met your expectations. We can't wait to welcome you back soon!" or "Your support means everything to us, [Customer Name]! We're so glad you enjoyed your experience. Let us know if we can do anything to improve it!"

If the review is negative, acknowledge the issue. Use empathy and accountability.

✔ **What to Say**: "Thank you for your feedback, [Customer Name]. We're sorry to hear about your experience."

✔ **What Not to Say**: Avoid defensive phrases like: "That's not true" or "You must be mistaken."

Apologize and Take Responsibility:

✔ **What to Say**: "We take your concerns seriously and want to resolve this issue. Please get in touch with us at [contact info]."

✔ **What Not to Say:** Don't use dismissive language like: "This isn't a big deal" or "It's not our fault."

Provide a Public Follow-Up (if resolved):

✔ **What to Say:** "Hi, [Customer Name]. We're glad we could connect and address your concerns. Your feedback helps us grow!"

Pro Tip: Develop a **response library** of pre-approved templates for common review scenarios (e.g., late delivery, service quality, etc.).

Step #4 – Respond Promptly

Another common mistake is delaying responses. One study found that **33% of customers expect a reply within three days**, while another cited that **53%** expect a response within seven days. Conversely, **bad reviews on X often expect a reply within one hour.**[51]

Assign response review duties to a dedicated team member or utilize AI tools to quickly draft replies. Additionally, inconsistent messaging across platforms can confuse or alienate customers. Maintaining a consistent tone, whether casual on Yelp or professional on LinkedIn, strengthens your brand identity and fosters confidence in your communication.

One of the best books I've read on dealing with negative online reviews is *Hug Your Haters: How to Embrace Complaints and Keep Your Customer* by Jay Baer. I highly recommend the book. It's a quick read, backed by in-depth research and packed with practical strategies to manage and recover from negative online complaints. Baer also recommends responding to every review up to two times.

IT'S ALL ABOUT THE ASK

Don't leave your online reputation to chance. Be strategic with how you ask your customers for feedback.

1. **Customize the survey questions (design and messaging) in your online reputation management software.** Default messages may come across as overly generic and bland. The wording in your survey and email messages should be friendly and personalized. Ensure the message conveys that you genuinely care about the fan and their experience.

2. **Check-in regularly and well before the transaction ends.** By checking in periodically, you won't be caught off guard by negative feedback at the conclusion of the sale. Train your front-line professionals to ask, "How are we doing so far?" At my local grocery store, however, they wait to ask, "Did you find everything you needed?" until I reach the checkout lane. By then, I no longer care about the items I couldn't find; I want to finish and leave! It would be much better if the store assigned a dedicated employee to roam the aisles, checking on shoppers and assisting them in finding whatever they need while shopping.

3. **Don't beg or pressure customers for a favorable review.** Praise must be earned. The opposite happens when a company states, "You'll receive a survey about our service today, and we would appreciate it if you could rate us a 10. Anything less than that, and the corporate office will deny our store the pizza party we've all dreamed of!" I hear this comment every time I visit my local drugstore, and I find it very off-putting. Fans generally do not want to be told what rating to give. Being instructed this way feels heavy-handed and manipulative.

4. **Don't bribe your fans for positive reviews.** Offering discounts, coupons, or free items in exchange for a positive online review is a serious mistake. Please avoid doing this! Yelp and Google have strict guidelines regarding false reviews and will not publish any review they consider to be artificially incentivized.

5. **Make It Easy.** Alongside offering automated survey software, consider providing simple options for satisfied customers to leave positive reviews. Include a link to your review sites in the signature line of your emails. Create links from your website

to your review platforms. Add links to review sites in mass marketing emails. Regularly share links to review sites on your social media. Finally, display the web addresses of review sites on window clings and signage if you operate a physical location.

Mastering your online reputation involves more than just responding to reviews or striving for the perfect star rating—it's about building trust, showcasing authenticity, and nurturing meaningful connections with your customers. **In today's digital age, your online reputation serves as your silent salesperson, your MX, influencing potential buyers long BEFORE they interact with you directly.** By proactively managing your presence, responding with empathy, and consistently refining your strategies, you can turn reviews into powerful tools for growth and loyalty. Remember, your brand is shaped not by what you say but by the experiences you create and the relationships you nurture. Stay engaged, stay authentic, and continue striving for lasting success.

THE BALL IS IN YOUR COURT—PRACTICE DRILL #13

Conduct a comprehensive audit of your online reputation. Start by Googling your business name and reviewing the first page of results. Explore key platforms like Google Business Profile, Yelp, and any industry-specific sites where customers might leave feedback. Take note of the number, recency, and tone of the reviews on each platform. Categorize feedback into themes: What do customers love about your business? What complaints or issues do you see repeatedly?

Next, evaluate how you're engaging with your reviews. Are you responding promptly and professionally? If not, develop a plan to improve response times and establish consistent messaging across platforms. Finally, identify gaps in your strategy: Are you asking customers for reviews effectively? Are there tools you could implement to automate and enhance your efforts? Write down three action steps you can take to build momentum in managing your online reputation.

Takeaway for Marketers: This drill empowers marketers to approach their online reputation strategically, turning customer feedback into a tool for growth and trust-building. By understanding what customers are saying and how they're responding, marketers gain the insights needed to refine their approach, engage effectively, and maintain a stellar reputation that drives customer loyalty and business success.

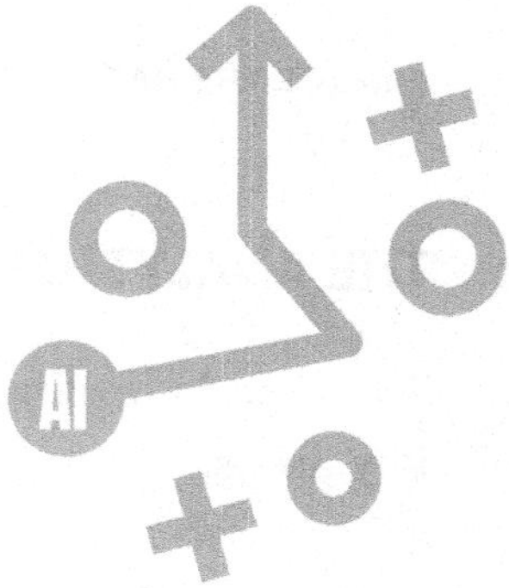

Secret #9

HALFTIME ADJUSTMENTS

Analyze and Reboot with Google Analytics 4 (GA4)

IN SPORTS, HALFTIME isn't just a break; it's a strategic moment to assess the first half, pinpoint what's effective, tackle what's ineffective, and adapt strategies to secure a victory. Similarly, in business, analytics serves the same purpose.

GA4 is your playbook, instant replay, and scoreboard—all in one.

With AI-powered tools, cross-platform tracking, and an emphasis on actionable insights, GA4 provides marketers with data-driven clarity. This chapter guides you in turning data into successful strategies and adapting in real time.

THE ANALYTICS SCORECARD—FIVE KEY FOCUS AREAS

To extract meaningful insights from GA4, you must focus on **five key areas.**

1. Your Audience—Know Who's in the Stands

Your audience is at the heart of your marketing strategy. GA4 helps you answer crucial questions about who they are, what they value, and how they engage with you.

Key Metrics to Track:

- **Demographics:** Age, gender, location, interests.
- **Devices Used:** Mobile, desktop, tablet.
- **New vs. Returning Users:** First-time visitors vs. loyal customers.
- **Active Hours:** When your audience is online.

Real-World Examples:

✔ A sporting goods retailer discovers that its primary audience consists of men aged 18-34, leading to a targeted campaign featuring high-performance workout gear.

✔ A meal kit delivery service learns that peak traffic occurs around 4 p.m., prompting them to schedule social media ads just before dinner time.

✔ A tech startup realizes that most of its returning users access the app on mobile, which inspires a mobile-first design refresh.

GA4 Report: Audience Overview

✔ **Where to Find It:** Reports > User > Demographics Overview.

✔ **What It Shows:** Key demographic data, user breakdown by device, and active hours.

***Pro Tip*:** Use demographic details to segment specific groups (e.g., mobile users aged 25-34).

2. Acquiring Website Traffic—Get Fans in the Seats

Traffic sources are your offensive strategy—the plays that bring people to your website or app.

Key Metrics to Track:

- **Traffic Sources:** Organic search, social media, paid ads, referrals.
- **Campaign Effectiveness:** Which campaigns deliver ROI?
- **Top Keywords:** What search terms bring visitors?
- **Cost Per Acquisition (CPA):** What's the ROI for each channel?

Real-World Examples:

✔ A nonprofit organization finds that Facebook drives most of its web traffic and doubles down on fundraising ads.

- ✔ A local bakery ranks highly for "wedding cakes near me" and invests in more wedding-related content.
- ✔ A tech consultancy firm discovers that email campaigns generate leads at half the cost of a paid search.

GA4 Report: Traffic Acquisition Report

- ✔ **Where to Find It:** Reports > Acquisition > Traffic Acquisition
- ✔ **What It Shows:** Breakdown of traffic by source/medium, campaign performance, and cost-per-lead (if integrated with Google Ads).

Pro Tip: Use Secondary Dimensions to see traffic performance by device or user type.

3. Driving Engagement—Keep the Crowd Cheering

Once users arrive, aim to capture their attention and keep them engaged. GA4 reveals what content resonates and where users drop off.

Key Metrics to Track:

- **Top-Performing Pages:** What content do users love?
- **Session Duration:** How long do users stay?
- **Click Behavior:** What buttons or CTAs are most popular?
- **Completion Rates:** Are users taking desired actions?

Real-World Examples:

✔ A homebuilder sees increased engagement on virtual home tours and invests more in high-quality video content.

✔ A financial advisor's blog notices that the time spent on "Retirement Planning" articles is extended, driving more content creation on similar topics.

✔ A real estate agency finds users frequently click the "View Homes" CTA, so it redesigned its site to highlight this button.

GA4 Report: Engagement Overview

✔ **Where to Find It:** Reports > Engagement > Engagement Overview

✔ **What It Shows:** Session durations, average engagement time, and top-performing content.

***Pro Tip*:** Use Engagement Details to see specific user actions on pages, like clicks or video plays.

4. Converting Leads—Seal the Victory

Traffic and engagement are great, but **conversions are where you score**. GA4 helps track and refine the user journey to maximize the number of goals completed.

Key Metrics to Track:

- **Goal Completions:** Purchases, form submissions, downloads.

- **Top Converting Traffic Sources:** Which channels drive the most actions?

- **Funnel Drop-Off Points:** Where do users abandon the process?

Real-World Examples:

✔ A car dealership finds Google Ads outperform social media for booking test drives and reallocates ad spend.

✔ A custom furniture retailer identifies drop-offs at the payment page and adds transparent shipping details earlier in the funnel.

✔ A fitness studio tracks free trial sign-ups as the primary conversion metric and optimizes campaigns to improve sign-up rates.

GA4 Report: Funnel Exploration Report

✔ **Where to Find It: Explore > Funnel Exploration**

✔ **What It Shows:** Visual representation of user drop-offs across key steps in the funnel.

***Pro Tip*:** Customize the funnel to match your unique conversion process (e.g., add steps like 'Cart > Checkout > Payment').

5. **Retention and Loyalty—Build a Dynasty Team**
Winning teams don't just attract fans—they **keep them coming back.** GA4 highlights loyalty drivers and churn risks.

Key Metrics to Track:

- **Return Rate:** How often users come back.
- **Loyalty Drivers:** Which features/content encourage return visits?
- **Churn Signals:** Predictive analytics to spot at-risk users.

Real-World Examples:

✔ A news website identifies weather updates as a top loyalty driver and expands weather features.

✔ A subscription box service notices repeat logins spike after monthly reminder emails.

✔ A software company uses predictive analytics to identify churn-risk users and targets them with personalized onboarding campaigns.

GA4 Report: Retention Report

✔ **Where to Find It:** Reports > Retention

✔ **What It Shows:** User retention trends, new vs. returning user behavior, and churn patterns.

***Pro Tip*:** Use **Predictive Metrics** to spot high-risk churn users before they leave.

FINAL WHISTLE: DATA DRIVES DECISIONS

GA4 offers the tools, but **you make the calls.** Understand your audience, optimize campaigns, refine engagement, and build loyalty. **The scoreboard is only valuable if you know how to use it.**

THE BALL IS IN YOUR COURT—PRACTICE DRILL #14

- ✓ **Objective:** Transform GA4 data into one actionable insight and adjustment.
- ✓ **Choose One Focus Area:** Select from Audience, Acquisition, Engagement, Conversion, or Retention.
- ✓ **Access the Appropriate Report:** Navigate to the relevant GA4 report (e.g., Traffic Acquisition, Engagement Overview, Retention Report).
- ✓ **Identify One Key Metric:** Spot a standout trend, anomaly, or top-performing statistic.
- ✓ **Discover One Insight:** Ask, "Why is this happening?" (e.g., "Traffic dropped due to outdated content.").
- ✓ **Implement One Action:** Based on your insight, plan a single improvement (e.g., "Update blog content to enhance SEO.").
- ✓ **Measure the Results:** Monitor changes after making your adjustment.

The Outcome: One clear insight, one strategic action, and measurable improvement.

Takeaway for Marketers: Raw data answers the question, '*What happened?*' Insights explain *'Why did it happen?'* and '*What will we do next?*' GA4 is more than just a tool—it's your navigator for more thoughtful decision-making. Focusing on five key areas, utilizing the correct reports, and prioritizing actionable insights will allow you to adapt your strategy in real time and drive measurable success. **Remember: Data is your scoreboard, but insights represent your winning strategy. Keep analyzing, keep adjusting, and keep scoring.**

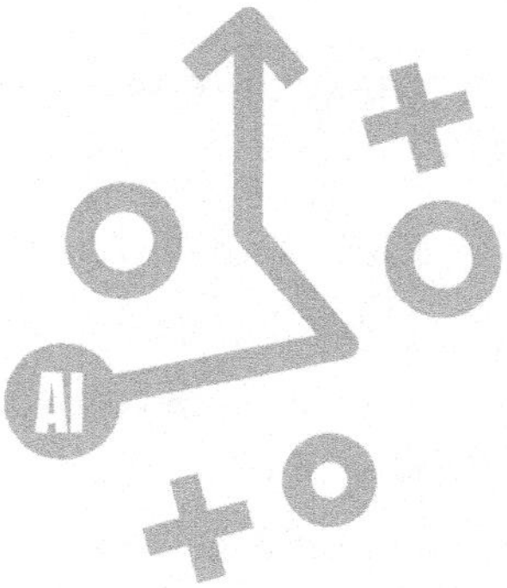

Secret #10

TAKE THE GLOVES OFF

Be a SuperFan of Your Fans

AT ITS CORE, great marketing is love in action. It embodies understanding, care, and responsiveness to your audience's needs. This book has explored the art and science of engaging your audience, embracing AI, and nurturing lasting connections. Now, as we conclude, it's time to turn up that passion to eleven: it's time to become a **SuperFan** of your fans.

In a world inundated with marketing messages, **authenticity is your secret weapon, and transparency is your currency of trust**. Fans can spot insincerity from a mile away. Being a SuperFan of your fans isn't about flashy campaigns or gimmicks—it's about showing up genuinely, humanizing your business, and fostering relationships grounded in mutual respect.

I learned two lessons from my mom that apply here. She spent years shaping young minds as a 12th-grade British Literature teacher and leading training classes for church educators. Growing up, I was her teaching assistant at church, observing her in action as she brought lessons to life through her genuine connection with her class. Among the many pearls of wisdom she shared, two lessons stand out—insights that resonate deeply in teaching, marketing, leadership, and life.

The first lesson was simple yet profound: "You can't give away what you don't have." My mom always said, "You can't pour love and care into others if your bucket is empty." As a teacher, she understood that if she arrived at her classroom exhausted, disconnected, or disengaged, her students would sense it immediately. She believed you must nurture yourself physically, mentally, and emotionally before giving to others. That's why we began with Secret #1—how modern marketers think, act, and feel.

This principle applies perfectly to marketing and leadership. If you're running on empty, your fans will notice. Your content will feel forced, your campaigns will lack passion, and your communication will become hollow. **Being a SuperFan of your fans begins with being a SuperFan of yourself—filling your bucket with inspiration, rest, and self-care so you can show up authentically and deliver your best.**

The second lesson came from one of her favorite stories: *The Velveteen Rabbit* by Margery Williams. My mom often concluded her training classes for church educators with a quote from this book. In this beloved tale, a stuffed rabbit becomes worn and tattered over time because he is deeply loved by his child owner.

The rabbit learns that being *real* isn't about being perfect—it's about being authentic, loved, and seen for who you truly are. In the book, the Skin Horse says: "Real isn't how you are made... It's a thing that happens to you. When a child loves you for a long, long time, not just to play with, but REALLY loves you, then you become Real."

In marketing, being *real* isn't about perfection—it's about **showing the people, stories, and moments behind your brand.** It's about letting your fans see the human side of your business. Your audience doesn't just want polished ads and curated social media posts—they want to know the people behind the logo, the heart behind the product, and the effort behind every campaign.

Being Real in Marketing Looks Like This:

- **Show Behind-the-Scenes Moments:** Share photos or videos of your team working, celebrating wins, or just being themselves. Let your fans see the people making the magic happen.

- **Introduce Your Team:** Highlight employees in your content—share their stories, passions, and contributions to your brand.

- **Celebrate Everyday Wins:** Not every moment needs to be a polished campaign. Sometimes, a snapshot of a team pizza party or a candid office moment resonates more than a professionally shot ad.

- **Be Transparent About Your Processes:** Show how your product is made, how your team brainstorms ideas, or how you pack orders for shipping.

When brands embrace these moments, they stop being faceless corporations and become relatable, human, and memorable. Just like the Velveteen Rabbit, they become **real**.

Before we say goodbye, let's reflect on what we've learned:

1. **Start with Empathy**—Pre-Season,

2. **Leverage Tools and Talent**—Play Ball!,

3. **Optimize and Adapt**—Charge the Back Nine,

4. **Celebrate and Appreciate**—Extra Innings, and,

5. **Be Transparent and Authentic**—Game-Changer.

What does superfandom look like for your business? Maybe it's recognizing your top customers with personalized thank-you notes. Perhaps it's engaging directly with followers on social media or hosting exclusive events to make them feel special.

- ✔ **Be Transparent:** Show behind-the-scenes moments, introduce your team, and share your processes.

- ✔ **Be Authentic:** Show your personality in your content, stay true to your brand values, and focus on connection over perfection.

- ✔ **Be Present:** Listen actively to your fans, respond thoughtfully, and create opportunities for two-way conversations.

Being a SuperFan of your fans is not a **tactic**; it's a **mindset**. It's the culmination of everything this book stands for—making marketing personal, powerful, and extraordinary.

As we close this chapter, I want to pause and share something personal with you.

I am your SUPERFAN.

Yes, you—the reader. I'm in your corner, cheering for your success and believing in your vision, even when the path feels uncertain or overwhelming. You've taken the time to dive into this book, invest in your growth, and expand your skills. That deserves recognition and celebration.

Everything you need to succeed is within your reach.

Whether you're a seasoned marketer or just beginning your journey, I believe you can create something FANtastic.

Now, let's play ball!

Part V

HOME FIELD ADVANTAGE

"Sure, home-field is an advantage, but so is having a lot of talent."

Dan Marino, Former NFL Quarterback, Miami Dolphins
Pro Football Hall of Famer

QUICK VIEW SUMMARY OF THE PRACTICE DRILLS

IN THIS SECTION, you'll find two helpful resources.

1. A summary of all the drills and exercises mentioned throughout this book is listed here for your convenience.

2. List of my tech tool equipment kit. These are the tools I use daily to brainstorm, communicate, design, and organize my role as the Chief Marketing Strategist at Meredith Communications.

First up: the practice drills. These exercises are designed to help you turn the strategies in this book into actionable results. FANtastic Marketing isn't just about learning—it's about doing. Take the time to work through these drills and start applying what you've learned. Implementation is the key to transforming insights into impact and seeing results.

PRACTICE DRILL #1

Consumers know when a brand connects to The *Power of We* and when it misses the mark. The next time you find yourself scratching your head at a television/streaming ad that doesn't make sense, think about why not. Was it the graphics, use of or lack of humor, the actors, or the message? Regardless of what aspect missed the mark, I guarantee it didn't appeal to you because it failed to make an emotional connection.

PRACTICE DRILL #2

Stop and take note the next time you feel a jolt of "I can do that!" from a marketing message. Identify a brand that boosts your self-esteem. Examine what aspects of the brand instill confidence in you and how its marketing communicates that empowering, aspirational message to potential customers.

PRACTICE DRILL #3

Identify your preferred escape activities. Is it reading a great book, binge-watching a series, or exercising? How do you feel during these escapes? Write down those feelings and notice when a product or service resonates with them. Effective marketing connects with these emotions to create a sense of relief or joy for its audience.

PRACTICE DRILL #4

Consider making a state change the next time you feel stuck in a rut or creatively blocked. Take a quick timeout to watch a funny cat video on YouTube, or go for a brisk walk outside. Try doing jumping jacks or turn up the music in your car. How do you feel afterward? What happens when you attempt to return to work?

PRACTICE DRILL #5

Make a list of the groups you belong to (both virtual and physical).

- What do you like about being a part of the group?
- What are the benefits to you mentally, emotionally, and physically?
- How would you feel if you could no longer be part of the group?

PRACTICE DRILL #6

To put the principles of Think, Act, and Feel into practice, dedicate time this week to the following drill:

1. **Think**—Conduct a brainstorming session with your team focused on curiosity. Choose one campaign and ask:
   a. What's working, and why?
   b. What's not working, and how can we test new ideas?
   c. Are there assumptions we haven't challenged?
   d. Write down every insight or question, no matter how minor.

2. **Act**—Select one area of improvement identified during the brainstorming session and take action. For example:
   a. Update the visuals or messaging of an ad campaign to better align with your fans' identity.
   b. Test a new audience segmentation strategy for email marketing.

3. **Feel**—Identify one recent setback or underperforming campaign and reframe it as a learning opportunity. What went wrong, and what did you learn? Document this as a "lesson log" to guide future decisions.

PRACTICE DRILL #7

Choose a task or challenge your business often encounters—something repetitive, time-consuming, or creative. Investigate two AI tools that claim to assist with this task. For instance, you might investigate AI tools for generating blog content, creating visuals, or analyzing customer feedback. Evaluate each tool using the same task and compare their outputs. Assess the tools based on the following criteria: ease of use, accuracy, relevance to your needs, and overall value for your business. Rate each tool on a scale from 1 to 5 in each category and select the one that aligns best with your goals.

PRACTICE DRILL #8

Choose a product or brand that doesn't appeal to you. You earn bonus points if this brand offers a product or service you believe wastes time or money—something you would never purchase or be interested in. Put aside your judgment of its worth or value. Examine the fan base for the product. Develop a demographic and psychographic profile of that fan. Then, assess the product's messaging and rate its marketing on a scale from 1 to 10. A score of 1 indicates no understanding of its fan base, while a score of 10 shows mastery in knowing its fans and delivering exactly what they want.

PRACTICE DRILL #9

Conduct a deep dive into your website's analytic reports. If you don't know how to interpret them, hire an expert to help you. Become familiar with your performance numbers. Set up automated reporting so that you receive the reports at least once a month. Take the time to review your reports or delegate this task to someone on your team.

PRACTICE DRILL #10

Draw a wagon wheel on a clean sheet of paper. Based on the findings from Steps #1 - #3 above, label the wheel's spokes with your current traffic drivers. Then, create a second wheel with new online and offline traffic drivers you plan to implement.

PRACTICE DRILL #11

Brainstorm with your team to identify creative, engaging content that humanizes your brand, highlights key partnerships, and showcases compelling visuals:

1. **Behind-the-Scenes Content**—Develop a list of behind-the-scenes moments to share on social media. Show how your products are made, introduce team members, or provide a sneak peek into your daily operations. Draw inspiration from brands like Disney, which excels at storytelling and self-revelation.

2. **Recognize VIPs**—Identify your Very Important Partners (VIPs), including vendors, collaborators, referrers, and community organizations. Create posts that spotlight their contributions and

celebrate their impact on your business. Publicly acknowledging these relationships fosters goodwill and strengthens your brand community.

3. **Plan Visual Assets**—Evaluate your need for visuals, such as product photos, testimonial videos, or event footage. Create a plan to consistently capture high-quality images and videos at key moments in your workflow. Organize these assets in a cloud-based library for easy access and ensure your team has a clear strategy for incorporating them into your marketing.

PRACTICE DRILL #12

Compile a comprehensive list of the questions most frequently asked by your fans. Include every question; none is too small or unimportant—list as many as possible. Afterward, review the list to eliminate duplicates. Organize the questions into categories by topic. Create a master FAQ document using Excel, Sheets, or Google Docs. When seeking inspiration for your content marketing, start with the questions on the list.

PRACTICE DRILL #13

Conduct a comprehensive audit of your online reputation. Start by Googling your business name and reviewing the first page of results. Explore key platforms like Google Business Profile, Yelp, and any industry-specific sites where customers might leave feedback. Take note of the number, recency, and tone of the reviews on each platform. Categorize feedback into themes: What do customers love about your business? What complaints or issues do you see repeatedly?

Next, evaluate how you're engaging with your reviews. Are you responding promptly and professionally? If not, develop a plan to improve response times and establish consistent messaging across platforms. Finally, identify gaps in your strategy: Are you asking customers for reviews effectively? Are there tools you could implement to automate and enhance your efforts? Write down three action steps you can take to build momentum in managing your online reputation.

PRACTICE DRILL #14

✔ **Objective:** Transform GA4 data into one actionable insight and adjustment.

✔ **Choose One Focus Area:** Select from Audience, Acquisition, Engagement, Conversion, or Retention.

✔ **Access the Appropriate Report:** Navigate to the relevant GA4 report (e.g., Traffic Acquisition, Engagement Overview, Retention Report).

✔ **Identify One Key Metric:** Spot a standout trend, anomaly, or top-performing statistic.

✔ **Discover One Insight:** Ask, "Why is this happening?" (e.g., "Traffic dropped due to outdated content.").

✔ **Implement One Action:** Based on your insight, plan a single improvement (e.g., "Update blog content to enhance SEO.").

✔ **Measure the Results:** Monitor changes after making your adjustment.

MEREDITH'S EQUIPMENT BAG: RECOMMENDED TOOLS

THESE ARE THE TOOLS I rely on daily, along with those used by our team, to achieve exceptional marketing results for our clients. Whether it's productivity, creativity, or AI-driven efficiency, each tool has earned its place in my equipment bag. This is not intended to be an exhaustive list, but rather a collection of the tools we use most frequently and in which we have the utmost confidence.

DESKTOP TOOLS

My go-to tools for productivity, communication, and content creation.

- **Calendly**—Scheduling made easy.**
- **Dropbox**—File storage and sharing.**
- **Google Calendar**—My time management hero.*
- **Google Docs and Sheets**—Cloud-based tools for word processing/spreadsheets.*
- **Google Drive**—Cloud-based collaboration hub.*

- **Grammarly**—AI-powered grammar, spelling, and style assistant.*
- **Mac Mail**—Efficient email management.
- **Loom**—Video messaging for effective communication.*
- **Keynote**—Presentation design.
- **MailChimp**—Email marketing campaigns.*
- **Microsoft Office for Mac**—Classic productivity suite.
- **Pages**—Apple's intuitive document creation tool.
- **ShareFile**—Secure document storage and sharing.
- **Slack**—Real-time team communication, collaboration, file storage, and task management.
- **Zoom**—Virtual meetings, webinars, and collaboration*

AI-FIRST TOOLS

These AI-powered tools help me automate tasks, generate insights, and optimize workflows.

- **ChatGPT 4o (Paid Version)**—This is my AI linebacker! While I use a few other AI tools listed below, I can achieve most of what I outlined in this book with ChatGPT.
- **Fathom**—AI-powered meeting summaries and insights.
- **Munch**—Intelligent content repurposing and social media optimization.
- **Ophaya Smart Pen**—Digitize and sync your handwritten notes.
- **Otter.ai**—AI-driven transcription and note-taking with accuracy.
- **Saleswise.ai**—AI-based sales insights and analytics.

CHROME EXTENSIONS

Quick tools I use directly from my Chrome browser for everyday tasks.

- **Awesome Screenshot**—Capture, annotate, and share your screen effortlessly.
- **Bit.ly**—Shorten, customize, and track URLs.
- **ColorZilla**—Pick colors and extract palettes.
- **Font Picker**—Identify and match fonts online.
- **LastPass**—Manage passwords securely.
- **Meta Pixel Helper**—Verify Facebook Pixel installation.
- **Pocket**—Save articles and videos for later viewing.
- **Rakuten, RetailMeNot, & Honey**—Use smart shopping and cashback tools.
- **Tag Assistant**—Verify and debug Google Tag Manager installations.

MEREDITH COMMUNICATIONS' TOOLS

Tools our team uses the most often deliver outstanding marketing results.

- **Adobe Illustrator**—Graphic design and illustration.*
- **Adobe Photoshop**—Photo editing and design.*
- **Adobe Stock Photo**—High-quality stock imagery.*
- **Canva***—Design tool for content creation.
- **Content Cloud**—Content planning and management.
- **CyberFortress**—Data protection and cybersecurity.
- **DashThis**—Digital marketing reporting dashboards.
- **Facebook Ad Manager***—Manage and optimize ad campaigns.
- **Facebook Business Manager**—Comprehensive account management.

- **Google Ad Manager***—Ad campaign optimization and tracking.
- **Google Analytics**—I'm not explaining what this is again, ha!
- **Google Business Profile**—Ditto!
- **Google Search Console**—Monitor and optimize website SEO.
- **Google Tag Manager**—Tag configuration and tracking setup.
- **iStock**—Professional stock photos and graphics.*
- **Linktree**—Link management for social media profiles.
- **Moz**—SEO analysis and optimization.
- **Yoast***—SEO plugin for content optimization.

These tools aren't just software—they're **extensions of my strategy, creativity, and efficiency.** Whether you're managing campaigns, crafting content, or analyzing results, this equipment bag is packed with the essentials to **work smarter, not harder.**

Let me know if there's a tool you love that I should add to my kit!

**Tools with an asterisk "*" include AI-powered, add-on features or integrate with AI 3rd Party Tools.*

***Tools with two asterisks "**" have AI-powered features coming soon.*

Part VI

EXTRA INNINGS

It's never over. You don't want to be in the position to be down four runs in the ninth inning, but it's not over until the last out.

Derek Jeter, Yankees All Time Career Leader in Hits, Doubles, Time on Base, Stolen Bases, Plate Appearances and At-Bats

HOW TO CONNECT WITH MEREDITH

MeredithCommunications.com
LinkedIn.com/in/MeredithOliver
Instagram: @MeredithComms
Facebook.com/MeredithCommunications
Facebook.com/BuilderTownHall
YouTube.com/MeredithOliverTV
X: @MereonMarketing

ENDNOTES

1 "Want to Chat with Flo? Progressive Announces New Auto Insurance Bot." *Progressive Insurance Media Room*, 17 Oct. 2017, progressive.mediaroom.com/2017-10-17-Want-to-chat-with-Flo-Progressive-Announces-New-Auto-Insurance-Bot.

2 "Progressive Launches Flo Chatbot." *Progressive Insurance Media Room*, 4 Feb. 2020, progressive.mediaroom.com/news-releases/?item=122478m.

3 "Stock Analysis." *Stock Analysis*, 1 Jan. 2025, stockanalysis.com/stocks/sfix/revenue/.

4 "Internet Use in 2024." *DataReportal*, 1 Jan. 2025, datareportal.com/reports/digital-2024-deep-dive-the-state-of-internet-adoption/.

5 Ch, David. "TikTok Statistics: Revenue & Usage (Updated Dec. 2024)." *Sendshort.Ai*, 15 Dec. 2024, sendshort.ai/statistics/tiktok/.

6 "'Brain Rot' Named Oxford Word of the Year 2024." *Oxford University Press*, 2 Dec. 2024, corp.oup.com/news/brain-rot-named-oxford-word-of-the-year-2024/.

7 "100+ Eye-opening Mobile Statistics for 2024." *Forms.App*, 27 Feb. 2024, forms.app/en/blog/mobile-statistics.

8 "Media multitasking." *Wikipedia*. 26 Oct. 2011. en.wikipedia.org/wiki/Media_multitasking.

9 "100+ Eye-Opening Mobile Statistics for 2024." *Forms.App*, 27 Feb. 2024, forms.app/en/blog/mobile-statistics.

10 "Media Multitasking is Really Multi-Distracting." *Science Daily*. 2 May 2011. sciencedaily.com/releases/2011/05/110502084444.htm.

11 "The Art of Fandom." *Anchorage Museum*, 1 Oct. 2017, anchoragemuseum.org/exhibits/the-art-of-fandom-2017/.

12 David C. "Reddit Stats." *Business of Apps,* 18 Oct. 2024, businessofapps.com/data/reddit-statistics/.

13 "Swing vote." *Wikipedia.* 11 Nov. 2011. en.wikipedia.org/wiki/Swing_vote.

14 Dowd, Matthew. "Karl Rove—The Architect." *UNC TV Frontline.* 12 April 2005. pbs.org/wgbh/pages/frontline/shows/architect/interviews/dowd.html - ixzz1SPUnoIKT.

15 Dannen, Chris. "How Obama Won It With The Web." *Fast Company.* 4 Nov. 2008. fastcompany.com/articles/2008/11/how-obama-won-it-with-the-web.html.

16 "First Findings Shed Light on Role of Social Media Algorithms in 2020 Election." *The University of Texas at Austin,* 23 Jul. 2023, moody.utexas.edu/news/socialmediainelections.

17 Frey, William. "Biden's Victory Came From the Suburbs." *Brookings,* 23 Jul. 2023, brookings.edu/articles/bidens-victory-came-from-the-suburbs/.

18 Hutchinson, Earl Ofari. "How Joe Can Win." *The Bay State Banner.* 27 August 2020. baystatebanner.com/2020/08/27/how-joe-can-win/.

19 Andrade, Sofia. "Women of Color Lead on the Ground in Georgia." *Who What Why.* 11 November 2020. whowhatwhy.org/politics/elections/women-of-color-lead-on-the-ground-in-georgia/.

20 Ashish, Dev. "Sports Fan Psychology: It's More Than Just a Game." *Bleacher Report.* 26 Sept. 2008. bleacherreport.com/articles/61709-sports-fan-psychology-its-more-than-just-a-game.

21 Ashish, Dev. "Sports Fan Psychology: It's More Than Just a Game." *Bleacher Report.* 26 Sept. 2008. bleacherreport.com/articles/61709-sports-fan-psychology-its-more-than-just-a-game.

22 "Speaking of Psychology: The Psychology of Sports Fans, with Daniel Wann, PhD." *American Psychological Association,* 1 Apr. 2024, apa.org/news/podcasts/speaking-of-psychology/sports-fans.

23 "Because You're Worth It." Loreal Paris USA, lorealparisusa.com/because-youre-worth-it.

24 Aslam, Salman. "Pinterest by the Numbers: Stats, Demographics, & Fun Facts." *Omnicore.* 10 January 2024. omnicoreagency.com/pinterest-statistics/.

25 Moore, Catherine. "What Is Eustress? A Look at the Psychology and Benefits." *Positive Psychology,* 15 Jan. 2019, positivepsychology.com/what-is-eustress/.

26 "What Is CBT?" *Beck Institute*, cares.beckinstitute.org/.

27 "Artificial Intelligence Market to Reach $1,811.75 Billion By 2030." *Grand View Research*, 1 May 2024, grandviewresearch.com/press-release/global-artificial-intelligence-ai-market.

28 "VALS Market Research." *SRI*, sri.com/hoi/vals-market-research/.

29 Haan, Katherine. "Top Website Statistics For 2024." *Forbes*, 4 Jun. 2024, forbes.com/advisor/business/software/website-statistics/.

30 Haan, Katherine. "Top Website Statistics For 2024." *Forbes*, 4 Jun. 2024, forbes.com/advisor/business/software/website-statistics/.

31 Haan, Katherine. "Top Website Statistics For 2024." *Forbes*, 4 Jun. 2024, forbes.com/advisor/business/software/website-statistics/.

32 "What Is Page Load Time and Why Is It Important?" *Big Commerce*, bigcommerce.com/glossary/page-load/.

33 Stillgoe, Dan. "Website Calls-to-action (CTA)—Examples and Best Practices." *Blend B2B*, 13 Jun. 2024, blendb2b.com/blog/website-call-to-action-cta-examples-and-best-practices.

34 "33 Impactful Social Proof Statistics (2024)." *Wiser Notify*, wisernotify.com/blog/social-proof-statistics/.

35 Rousseau, Olivier. "11 Simple Changes That Will Skyrocket Your Registration Form Conversions." *Activity Messenger*, 11 Sept. 2024, activitymessenger.com/blog/11-simple-changes-that-will-skyrocket-your-registration-form-conversions/.

36 Haan, Katherine. "Top Website Statistics For 2024." *Forbes*, 4 Jun. 2024, forbes.com/advisor/business/software/website-statistics/.

37 Haan, Katherine. "Top Website Statistics For 2024." *Forbes*, 4 Jun. 2024, forbes.com/advisor/business/software/website-statistics/.

38 "9 Importance of Product Photography Statistics in Ecommerce." *Business Dasher*, 4 Nov. 2024, businessdasher.com/product-photography-statistics/.

39 "Why Does a Small Business Need Business Analytics." *Sontai*, 19 Nov. 2024, sontai.com/post/why-does-a-small-business-need-business-analytics.

40 Gottfried, Jeffrey. "Americans' Social Media Use." *Pew Research Center*, 31 Jan. 2024, pewresearch.org/internet/2024/01/31/americans-social-media-use/.

41 Tuite, Harriet. "30 Stats That Prove the Benefits of Using Infographics." *Embryo*, 6 Jun. 2023, embryo.com/blog/30-stats-that-prove-the-benefits-of-using-infographics/.

42 Gottfried, Jeffrey. "23 PR & Press Release Statistics for Small Businesses." *Fit Small Business*, 16 Oct. 2024, pewresearch.org/internet/2024/01/31/americans-social-media-use/.

43 "2024 Blogging Statistics, Trends & Data – Ultimate List (UPDATED)." *Wpbeginner*, 18 Nov. 2024, wpbeginner.com/research/2022-blogging-statistics-trends-data-ultimate-list-updated.

44 Think Thing - Poly Design. "Do People Read Fully on the Web?" *LinkedIn Pulse*, 7 May 2024, linkedin.com/pulse/do-people-read-fully-web-pldsgnstudio-tvtoc/.

45 "Online Reviews Statistics." *Capital One Shopping*, 29 Oct. 2024, capitaloneshopping.com/research/online-reviews-statistics/.

46 Online Reviews Statistics." *Capital One Shopping*, 29 Oct. 2024, capitaloneshopping.com/research/online-reviews-statistics/.

47 "Reputation Marketing." *Wikipedia*, en.wikipedia.org/wiki/Reputation_marketing.

48 Clark, Jon. "18 Online Review Statistics Every Marketer Should Know." *Search Engine Journal*, 7 Nov. 2024, searchenginejournal.com/online-review-statistics/329701/.

49 "Online Reviews Statistics." *Capital One Shopping*, 29 Oct. 2024, capitaloneshopping.com/research/online-reviews-statistics/.

50 "Online Reviews Statistics." *Capital One Shopping*, 29 Oct. 2024, capitaloneshopping.com/research/online-reviews-statistics/.

51 "Online Reviews Statistics." *Capital One Shopping*, 29 Oct. 2024, capitaloneshopping.com/research/online-reviews-statistics/.

Made in the USA
Monee, IL
08 November 2026

67971945R00135